Portfolio Assessment: Getting Started

by Allan A. De Fina

SCHOLASTIC
PROFESSIONAL **B**OOKS

NEW YORK ◆ TORONTO ◆ LONDON ◆ AUCKLAND ◆ SYDNEY

Cover design by Vincent Ceci and Drew Hires
Design by Boultinghouse and Boultinghouse

ISBN   0-590-49183-0

12 11 10 9 8 7 6 5 4 3   3 4 5/9

Printed in the U. S. A.

Dedication

To my mentors and friends

Trika Smith-Burke
Bernice Cullinan
Willavene Wolf
Angela Jaggar
and
Lenore Ringler

Thanks for helping me be
the center of my own education.

Contents

Acknowledgments

I would like to thank the following people for their confidence in me and their support of me during the writing of this book. My mentors, Trika Smith-Burke, Bee Cullinan, Willavene Wolf, Angela Jaggar, and Lenore Ringler, have guided me in directing my interests and suggesting avenues of research. My editor at Scholastic, Terry Cooper, also showed tremendous confidence in my abilities and provided unceasing encouragement and support to me, both professionally and personally. I am especially grateful to my father, brother, and sister for letting me draw from their strength throughout my work. My friends and colleagues, Ro Pietranera, Ronnie Dalstrom, Laura Segal, Michael Stanziale, Lucy Di Maulo, Kathy Milk, Chris Maieran, Arturo Jimenez, David Treece, Lori and Gary Wolf, Druett Cameron, Shirley Matthews, David McGowan, Joan Rafter, Scott Herness, Henry J. Wong, Jo Bruno, Rich Sentipal, John McDonough, Charles Taylor, Gary Rocchio, Bob Davis, Joseph Ong, Mildred Gerestant, Russell Craig, Ray Ruiz, Susan Mernit, Patrick Moriarty, Arike Shaun Dyer, Linda Anstendig, Kathryn De Lawter, many of my students at AHM, NYU, Pace University, SUNY, and JCSC (especially my research assistants, Cristina Phaedonos and Kim Funderberg), my erstwhile and extremely tolerant administrators, Dr. Fred Means, Constance Clerk, Dennis Paporello, and Elaine Iberer, and the rest of my colleagues at AHM (especially my lunch mates, Sr. Jane Norton, Pat Holzman, Pat Murphy, Lori Bierig, and Ann Russell) many of whom read and made comments on various parts of the manuscript, and all of whom had faith in me, put up with my moments of madness and moodiness, and offered continuous support and encouragement. These wonderful people, along with so many others, remind me of Yeat's words, "Count where man's glory most begins and ends, and say my glory was I had such friends."

Many thanks are due the professionals who spent time sharing their experiences and materials about portfolio assessment. Without their assistance, much of the information in this book would have been merely theoretical, rather than practical. I am grateful to the following individuals for their generous help: Mayra Barrs, Centre for Language in Primary Education, London, England; Deborah Blanchard, Jordan-Small School, Raymond, ME; Kate Calfee, Palo Alto School District, Escondido, CA; Annie Calkins, Director of Curriculum and Assessment, Juneau School District, Juneau, AK; Adele Fiderer, Judith Abelove, Ellen Anders, Lila Berger, Ellen Citron, Judith D'Amore, Mary Hayter, and Ethel Huttar, Scarsdale Public Schools, Scarsdale, NY; Michael P. Ford, University of Wisconsin, Oshkosh, WI, and Marilyn M. Ohlhausen, University of Nevada, Las Vegas, NV; Rebecca P. Harlin and Stephen Phelps, State University of New York at Buffalo, NY; Cecilia Hysmith, Principal, Blackburn Elementary School, Manatee County, FL; Don Kemp, San Dieguito Union High School District, Encitas, CA; Linda Leonard Lamme, University of Florida, Gainesville, FL; Diane Lapp and James Flood, San Diego State University, San Diego, CA; Jackie Matthews, Orange County Public Schools, Orlando, FL; Allan Olson, Northwest Evaluation Association, Lake Oswego, OR; Liz Rand, Vermont State Department of Education, Montpelier, VT; Jean K. Rayer, Mainz American Elementary School, USMCA; Linda Rief, Oyster River Middle School, Durham, NH; Mary Roe, University of Delaware; Julie S. Ryan, Escondido Elementary School, Stanford, CA; Ginny Unane, Magnolia Elementary School; Carlsbad Unified School District, Carlsbad, CA; Maria Valeri-Gold, Division of Developmental Studies, Georgia State University, Atlanta, GA; Kenneth P. Wolf, Stanford University, Stanford, CA.

There were other anonymous individuals whose ideas helped shape my own. I wish to acknowledge the influence of their contributions, though I cannot personally acknowledge them. Finally, I apologize to any individuals whose names may have inadvertently been omitted from this list. I will endeavor to acknowledge these persons whenever and wherever possible.

Allan A. De Fina
May, 1992

Foreword

I realized early in my career that students experienced optimal learning when I allowed my assessment methodology to shape my teaching. In doing this, assessment provided information that was directly useful in forming decisions about teaching and learning for my students. For assessment to provide this type of information it has to be a process in nature that takes advantage of both subjective and objective evaluation. This is best achieved when the students are examined in a variety of contexts as well as by determining not only what a child has learned but how a child is learning. (Wooton, 1991, p. 3)

This statement made by a classroom teacher clearly indicates the direction in which assessment needs to go. Teachers are all too familiar with the inadequacies of standardized tests. How often have you heard a teacher say, "That test didn't measure how well Jessie understands what she reads. I know she reads better than that. I'm with her every day." It is this type of assessment made by the teacher in the context of "real" literacy experiences that should inform our curricular and instructional decisions.

Taylor (1991) in a recent article talks about assessment from the child's perspective. She describes an attempt to get as close as we can to the child's point of view. It involves observation of individual children as they work at reading and writing. It means giving them real opportunities to use language, and it provides us with information that is based upon observable literacy behaviors. This is in direct contrast to the call for more centralized type assessments. For example, the National Assessment of Educational Progress (NAEP) program is considering the expansion of normative testing. It is heartening, therefore, to hear a superintendent of schools (Monroe, 1991) state that current assessment practices present a narrow and confining view of children and a narrow and confining perspective on learning and teaching. He recommends instead that a program of assessment require that the teacher be the principal assessor, that the classroom be the context of assessment, and that it be formative rather than summative. As Chittenden and Courtney (1989) note, we do not need better tests to estimate students' relative status; instead we need assessment techniques that bring out the links between emerging skills and the foundations of literacy.

Is that what portfolio assessment is or is it just an additional word for our repertoire of educational jargon? Classroom observation indicates that portfolio assessment offers teachers a tool that is context-responsive. It gives teachers valuable information about what children know and can do; in particular, it provides information about the way language is used in reading and writing within different contexts. Most importantly, that information can be used immediately to inform instruction. Equally important is the fact that not only can the data be used by teachers but it can become a valuable tool for peer evaluation, for parent conferences, and for school administrators.

Portfolio assessment is a systematic process that continually changes as learners grow and develop their literacy skills. According to Sulzby (1990), portfolios are collections of children's "work" for the purpose of demonstrating progress. She believes that portfolios are particularly promising because children can be primarily responsible, with teacher guidance, in helping to keep track of what they are learning and mastering. She adds, however, that portfolios can only work if the teacher has the knowledge to help children build them and if the teacher can interpret the child's progress and development.

Offered in this book are ideas that will enable teachers to understand the rationale behind portfolio assessment, specific techniques to build portfolios, and ways of using students' work to assess their growth. The inclusion in this book of specific reading and writing activities which then can be used to diagnose students' literacy skills and plan appropriate instructional strategies is particularly powerful. It is important to note that data is collected on a ongoing basis and that instructional decisions are a collaboration between teachers and learners as they actively evaluate what is being learned. In this way, learners become self-critical, question their own learning, and set their own goals.

Allan De Fina, who is both a classroom teacher and a teacher educator, provides detailed information either to help you get started or to expand what you are already doing. In the case of a new teacher or a teacher who has previously relied on standardized test scores, the numerous examples and charts will give you the specifics you need to assess your students' reading and writing abilities as a part of your instructional program. For the more experienced teacher, this book should expand your repertoire of assessment techniques, thus giving you even more knowledge about your students' use of language as they read and write.

Underlying all of Allan's work is his philosophy that children are active learners, that classrooms need to encourage critical thinking, and that empowering students to question themselves, their peers, and their teachers will lead to improved literacy in this country. In putting this book together Allan gathered models of portfolios from teachers in classrooms across these United States. His contributors have used portfolios as a means of assessment with students of varying ages and abilities and from multi-ethnic backgrounds. Their examples provide clear evidence that portfolio assessment is limited only by the commitment of the teacher to an alternative form of assessment and not by the characteristics of the learners in the classroom. There are, however, problems that arise when teachers use portfolios for the purpose of assessment. Allan raises such issues as time management, the subjectivity of interpretation, and the transferability of information. It is one of the strengths of this book that he addresses both the positive aspects of using portfolios for assessment and the problems that teachers have found as they work with implementing portfolio assessment in a variety of classroom settings.

Portfolio Assessment: Getting Started is a major contribution to the field of literacy education. Teachers using the ideas in this book can change what happens in classrooms. Although change is a slow process, it begins with teacher and students working together in a supportive environment.

Lenore H. Ringler
New York University
Past President, NRC
May 1992

References

Chittenden, E. and Courtney, R. (1989). Assessment of young children's reading: Documentation as an alternative to testing. In D. S. Strickland and L. M. Morrow (Eds.), *Emerging literacy: Young children learn to read and write* (pp. 107–120). Newark, DE: International Reading Association.

Monroe, D. (1991). Qualities of a school district culture that support a dynamic process of assessment. In J. A. Roderick (Ed.), *Context-responsive approaches to assessing children's language* (pp. 97–104). Urbana, IL: National Conference on Research in English.

Sulzby, E. (1990, April). *Writing and reading instruction and assessment for young children: Issues and implications.* Paper commissioned by the Forum on the Future of Children and Families of the National Academy of Sciences and the National Association of State Boards of Education. Ann Arbor, MI.

Taylor, D. (1991). From the child's point of view: Alternate approaches to assessment. In J. A. Roderick (Ed.), *Context-responsive approaches to assessing children's language* (pp. 32–51). Urbana, IL: National Conference on Research in English.

Wooton, D. (1991). Vision in assessment: A testimony of progress in process. Unpublished manuscript, New York University.

1 Understanding Portfolio Assessment

Although portfolio assessment is relatively new to the classroom, it has been around for a long time. Artists and photographers, for example, often showcase their best works in a portfolio. Their portfolios—which may contain everything from sketches, slides, and photographs to exhibition announcements and newspaper or magazine reviews of art shows—are always the centerpiece for any presentation or discussion of their work with prospective employers or customers.

Journalists are perhaps the best example of how the use of portfolios can be transferred from the workplace to the classroom. Newspaper and magazine writers routinely keep a scrapbook of clippings of their publications. The articles, which fill the scrapbook's pages, show the diversity of a journalist's ability to write everything from news stories, feature articles, and interviews to pieces collaboratively written with colleagues. These portfolio entries not only show a writer's abilities but also reveal his or her growth as a writer.

How do these professionals determine what works should be placed in their portfolios? With expertise gained from education, from teacher and peer review, and mostly from self-evaluation, artists, photographers, and journalists come to know what is their best work and what is most valued by the experts in their fields. Their ability to be self-evaluative does not come overnight, of course. It is through years of study, discussion, and reflection upon their work that lists of criteria are developed—lists by which these professionals measure themselves.

If you are reading this book, you probably already see how these professional portfolios can have a direct application to education, but you also probably need a lot more information before you would even think about implementing portfolios into your classroom. The purpose of this book, therefore, is to help you understand the background, the rationale, and how-tos of portfolio assessment. What's more, this book will help you to get started using portfolios by showing you how to incorporate into portfolios many of the things you are already doing in your classroom.

Before you continue reading, though, it would be helpful if you took a few minutes to think about what you've already heard about portfolios so that you can confirm, change, and/or add to what you already know. Following are several frequently asked questions about portfolio assessment. Jot down some quick responses, and then you may want to keep your notes handy so that periodically, as you read through this book, you can reflect upon your thoughts and see how, if at all, your thinking about portfolios may have changed.

- ♦ What is portfolio assessment?
- ♦ Why do you need portfolio assessment?
- ♦ How is portfolio assessment different from traditional forms of assessment?
- ♦ What kinds of things are assessed using the portfolio approach?
- ♦ What kinds of assessment materials are placed in the portfolio?
- ♦ Who decides what goes into the portfolio?
- ♦ What are the problems with portfolio assessment?

There are no universal, simple answers to the questions just posed; instead, there are many answers to these questions, and each response will be slightly different, depending upon whom you ask. This book will provide you with some of the answers given by teachers who are presently using portfolios in their classrooms. Then, from the many ideas presented, you will be able to pick and choose those answers that best meet your individual needs.

Before going further, however, you need to understand an important distinction: there is a difference between portfolios themselves and portfolio assessment. Portfolios are the means by which assessments are made. Traditionally, tests have been the means by which assessments have been made, but you will see how portfolios can provide you with an alternative way—or an additional way—of examining students' strengths and weaknesses. In the process, you probably will also discover that by looking at actual student work over a period of time, you will have a clearer picture of what your students have learned than you ever could have by simply looking at some short answers on a test paper.

Assumptions About Portfolios

There are many definitions of portfolio assessment. Each definition, however, reflects the way portfolios are shaped by the individuals using them. While it may cause some consternation to know that there is no single, working definition, it should also be comforting to see that there's flexibility to expand the definition of portfolios to meet a variety of needs. There are, nevertheless, a set of assumptions that can be made about all portfolio assessment.

◆ **Portfolios are systematic, purposeful, and meaningful collections of students' works in one or more subject areas.**

A portfolio is not a collection of a student's work haphazardly thrown together, and it is not merely a writing folder into which a student's compositions for the school year are placed. A portfolio is a systematic compilation of a student's work. During this process of collecting, students make decisions about what pieces get placed into the portfolio, and it is this decision-making process that actually builds student involvement in their education. Keep in mind, though, that all items selected and placed into the portfolio should have some clear relevancy to the students' lives.

◆ **Students of any age or grade level can learn not only to select pieces to be placed into their portfolios but can also learn to establish criteria for their selections.**

Since the primary owners of the portfolios are students, they should be the ones to decide what items are placed into the portfolios, but they must also base their decisions on some clearly formulated criteria. Of course, your role as a teacher is to help them identify the criteria, provide models, and encourage them to continuously refine their criteria. The established criteria, then, should be spelled out somewhere in the portfolio so that anyone looking through it could understand what thinking was behind the decision to place a particular item into the portfolio. Students also should have the right to change their minds about pieces in their collections and remove them at any time.

◆ **Portfolio collections may include input by teachers, parents, peers, and school administrators.**

An essential participant in every portfolio is you, the teacher. However, your role will be more of a collaborator than an overseer. Together, for example, you and your students will brainstorm and debate criteria to be used in deciding which items will be placed in the portfolio. Peer commentary, evaluation, and suggestions are also welcome and, if possible, parents should also share in the creation of the portfolio by giving comments and reviewing pieces.

School administrations may even be a part of the portfolio compilation process. For example, some school principals and/or superintendents, eager to move away from standardized tests as the sole measure for evaluating students, may suggest the use of checklists and/or other evaluative criteria as part of the portfolio.

While an institutionalization of portfolios would not be advantageous because it takes empowerment away from the student and teacher, some criteria may be helpful if they are relevant to the student's purpose and if they supplement or replace standardized testing.

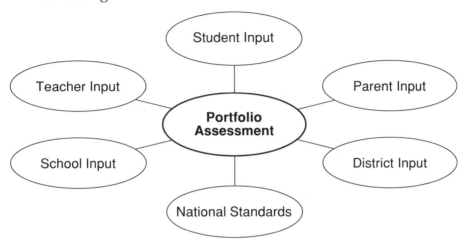

◆ **In all cases, portfolios should reflect the actual day-to-day learning activities of students.**

Portfolios should never be used to present a curriculum. Instead, they should be used to showcase what students have learned. In other words, they are not so much a measure of where students are going, but more a measure of where they have been and what they have accomplished.

◆ **Portfolios should be ongoing so that they show the students' efforts, progress, and achievements over a period of time.**

The portfolio should reflect a student's work over a period of time so that growth can be observed. Unlike tests, which provide only a glimpse of a student's work at a particular point in time, portfolios allow for a view of a student's work across time, task, subject, and style. Ideally, the portfolio should be passed on from grade level to grade level.

◆

◆ **Portfolios may contain several compartments, or subfolders.**

Since portfolios serve as repositories, it is possible that students may want to separate their best pieces from other pieces that are still in progress. Some teachers have recommended that there should be several compartments to the portfolio: one section for works in progress, another for notes and comments about the collected works, and one to showcase the best works. This last section would be for works that are polished—works that are meant to be seen and admired by the public.

Also, portfolios are not necessarily always file folders. Rather, they can be boxes, drawers in a cabinet, cubbies in a cubbyhole shelf, scrapbooks, or binders. Their sizes, shapes, and locations are determined only by the physical limitations of your classroom.

◆ **Selected works in portfolios may be in a variety of media and may be multidimensional.**

Although portfolios will always contain a lot of written works, students—if given the opportunity—might also want to include such things as items of personal significance, art work, dioramas, journals, and tape recordings. Any and all of these items are valuable if they reveal something about your students and their growth throughout the year.

As you read the following chapters, keep in mind that portfolio assessment can be used across all content areas of the curriculum. For example, math, science, and social studies portfolios are being used in some schools where these subjects are taught as separate parts of the curriculum. But, in many schools today, as the curriculum becomes more integrated and student centered, content-area subjects are routinely incorporated into and evaluated with the other contents of the portfolio. However, the remaining chapters of this book will discuss portfolios mainly as they relate to the reading and writing processes.

2 Getting Started

Imagine a classroom in which children want to learn and are always busily engaged in learning tasks. There is a buzz of excitement as they select books and materials, talk with peers about what they are reading and the projects they are working on, and seek out comments and suggestions about works in progress. It seems odd to think that anyone would want a classroom structured in any other manner than the one just described; but for years classroom life has practically been the opposite of this. Books were neatly shelved and removed only at scheduled times of the day, children completed assigned worksheets and text pages alone while quietly seated at their desks, and the desks were sometimes even bolted to the floor so that the children could not move around!

In many places all that has changed now because some educators realize that students need to believe that what they are doing is worthwhile. The commitment these educators have doesn't mean that their students have the run of the classroom, but they believe that their students should have the run of the curriculum. In other words, after the curriculum has been defined—based on the needs and interests of the students, the insights of the teacher, and the guidelines established by the school district and refined as an ongoing process—students are invited to make decisions about how best to undertake the tasks they have set as goals before them. To evaluate whether or not they have reached their goals, students are even asked to suggest ways to measure what they have learned. Initially, of course, students need some guidance with these tasks because establishing purposeful goals, thinking about the best ways to attain those goals, and learning to evaluate how well those goals have been met are all processes that take time to develop. It is in such an environment that portfolios can be used to their fullest potential.

Practical Suggestions for Getting Started

There's an old adage that says in order to try something new, it's necessary to give up something else. Teachers everywhere would probably disagree because more often than not they have to keep adding more things to their already lengthy list of duties and responsibilities, but they rarely get a chance to remove anything from that same list. Initially, using portfolios in the classroom will also require additional time as you work out how to give more responsibility for activities and assessment to your students. Once fully under way, you will be delighted to find out that using portfolios may actually give you more time to get other things done!

Following are some suggestions for effectively implementing portfolio use and assessment into your daily classroom routine.

1. Explain and Educate

Before getting started, take the time to win the support of your principal and/or curriculum supervisor. Be prepared to answer questions about portfolio assessment and, if possible, pass on the name of a school in your city or state that has successfully implemented the use of portfolios. If you have the backing of your school administration, you will be able to accomplish more in a shorter period of time, and you also might find that other teachers in your school will be encouraged to experiment with portfolios as well.

Many parents will become willing partners in—and powerful advocates of—portfolio assessment if you also ask them to become participants in the portfolio process. Initially, if possible, schedule meetings with individuals or small groups of parents and describe how portfolio assessment works and why it is such a wonderful method of evaluation. Informative, but not technical, newsletters sent home will also familiarize parents with the hows and whys of portfolio compilation and assessment. Then invite parents to share in the reviewing and evaluating of their children's portfolios.

Once you have the green light to go ahead, you will also need to explain to your students that you are going to try something new and exciting. You might want to tell them, for example, that you are going to be asking them to start making some important decisions about their own work. In other words, they will be sharing some of the responsibility for evaluation of their work. Providing models of portfolios, discussing them, and explaining the reasoning behind compiling a portfolio are other important steps to take before actually launching your own program.

2. Decide How-To and When

Prepare a phase-in schedule so that you don't overwhelm yourself—or your students—by trying to do too much all at once. For instance, it may take you some time and planning just to settle on where and how to keep the portfolios. If you have more than one class, you also may want to consider implementing portfolio use with only one class and then gradually adding the others.

In each class, begin by choosing one or two areas where portfolios will naturally fit in with the kinds of activities you are currently doing. For example, portfolio accumulation could very easily begin as part of reading or writing activities. Reading logs, literature reviews, self-reflective checklists, writing samples, and/or grammatical checklists could be incorporated without extensive preparation. (*Additional examples of portfolio entries are provided in this chapter, starting on page 23.*)

3. Demonstrate and Decide

Discuss with your students what kinds of things they'd like to include in their portfolios. Initially, if you are able to show your students actual working examples of portfolios, you will give them a concrete basis to accept, reject, and react to. It's not necessary, of course, for all students to agree on which items should be included. In fact, students should be able to choose and suggest items to customize their portfolios. You can even have a contract ready for students to sign so that you and they know and remember exactly what was agreed upon. Keep in mind, as well, that what goes into a portfolio will always vary, depending on the level and abilities of your students.

4. Establish a Grading Policy

Consider how your grading policy will be affected by the use of portfolios. You may need to meet with your principal and/or curriculum supervisor to discuss the implications of portfolio assessment upon traditional grading policy. (*For more information about alternative grading, see Chapter 3, pages 37–39.*)

5. Rethink Your Environment

You will, of course, have to designate a space within your classroom for storing your students' portfolios. As you make plans, keep in mind that your students will become more actively involved in compiling their portfolios if they have both time and space available for reviewing them.

Ideally, it also would be nice if you had enough space in your classroom to accommodate various portfolio activities such as a book reading and review center, a project work area, a research/content materials library and media resource center, a conference area—for individual and small-group conferencing—an audio/video taping center, and an arts and crafts center.

However, you can have a highly successful portfolio program without a single one of these additions.

6. Organize

Organize groups and group activities and, if necessary, establish a flexible schedule for moving through the various group-work areas of the classroom. As your students become accustomed to the expectations of group work, allow them to choose group projects or aspects of group projects and permit them to choose group members. Designate or have students designate particular group members to oversee compilation and/or presentation of group projects. Of course, as your students work in groups, you can schedule in some conferences with individual students.

7. Schedule

Set up specific times for direct instruction, large-group discussions, individual conferences, and the time you will need to evaluate student work, write notes, plan, and select materials.

If all of these suggestions seem overwhelming and time consuming, keep in mind—and be inspired by—the four surprises that Margie Krest had when she began to use portfolios in her classroom [*English Journal*, Feb. 1990].

1. I lightened my paper load.
2. I spent more time coaching students rather than grading them.
3. I began looking forward to grading students' papers (at least I became excited about how an idea or revision turned out).
4. Most important, I watched as previously unmotivated writers became motivated to work for a grade they desired and at the same time to improve their writing.

Looking Inside the Portfolio

There are two compelling considerations to keep in mind when deciding the contents of a portfolio: the owner's wishes and the purpose for collecting each item. Ideally, the portfolio should be as student centered as possible. By asking your students to make decisions about the selection and quality of their work, they begin to establish standards by which their work can be evaluated. Knowing the purpose for saving particular pieces of work over other pieces also helps them delineate criteria for judgment. Your students, for example, will soon begin to recognize that some work samples do not demonstrate certain desired qualities, and since they naturally want to show their best work, they will begin to carefully choose items for inclusion or showcasing. Even the process of choosing what to include in the portfolio is a metacognitive process.

Of course, many teachers have materials they would like included in students' portfolios as well. In many schools, some portfolio assessment checklists are even mandated by school administrations and/or by district authorities. Helping your students understand the reasons why some items must be placed in their portfolios can be a part of their learning experience. Whenever possible, however, incorporating materials through discussion, rather than by imposing them on your students, is an excellent way to develop trust between you and them.

Placing Items in Portfolios

Many different kinds of items can be placed in portfolios. Most will be student-generated items like essays, book reports, short stories, etc., but there may also be some ready-made items like checklists and forms that can be easily filled out and used later as a part of the evaluative process. The following list, however, may be helpful when you and your students are making decisions about which items to include in their portfolios. For each of the suggested activities, some descriptions of materials/task and a limited number of assessment possibilities are provided. Of course, the number of ways in which work samples may be evaluated is limited only by the specifications of the tasks themselves.

◆ **Essays and Reports**

Including different kinds of essays in portfolios provides you with information about your students' understanding of various genre and their ability to write using a variety of styles. Reports also demonstrate your students' research abilities, organizational skills, understanding of material, and sense of reportorial style.

◆ **Letters**

All types of letters indicate your students' knowledge of audience, purpose, and format. Additionally, grammar and punctuation skills are easily assessed in these short contexts.

◆ **Poetry and Other Creative Writing**

Whether a short story or a poem, these creative kinds of works may serve to demonstrate your students' imaginations, metaphorical thinking, and ability to use language vividly. Students poetry may also represent their understanding of poetic forms and figurative language and their ability to adopt alternate writing forms.

◆ **Sequels/Spin-Offs**

These responses to text demonstrate your students' use of imagination, comprehension of story line, understanding of characterization, and their ability to make predictions and to establish continuity or relatedness of theme(s).

◆ **Problem Statements/Solutions**

Asking students to restate, either orally or by writing, a problem encountered in text and to identify its solution—or to formulate a hypothesis and to predict its conclusion—provides assessment of your students' comprehension and reasoning abilities. Furthermore, in such situations, you should be able to evaluate your students' use of certain reading strategies—such as their ability to predict and confirm/disconfirm.

◆ Response Logs/Reviews

These items are usually written in a freestyle by your students in response to something they have read. To help them get started, ask them to respond to specific questions about a particular text. Your questions should be those types that stimulate critical thinking and reflection about the text. Their responses will provide information about their comprehension and appreciation of texts of various genre.

◆ Journal Entries

Journal entries are usually less structured and are not necessarily related to your students' schoolwork. Dialogue journals and peer response journals are two types of frequently used journals. Dialogue journals are written exchanges, usually between you and your students, in which both writers introduce whatever topics they choose. In peer response journals, students become classroom pen pals. These types of journals allow your students to express their ideas and opinions while providing insight into their writing abilities, thought processes, and cognitive development.

◆ Interviews

Pairs of students may interview each other about background knowledge of a subject, opinion on a topic, or response to something they have read. Interviewing allows them to develop their use of higher level question- answer relationships. Critical thinking and analysis are necessary to develop and respond to the questions and to maintain the dialogue. You can observe, record, and evaluate the quality of the interview as it occurs or assess the interview in a transcribed form.

◆ Posters/Artistic Media

Illustrations, dioramas, maps, photography, comic strips, etc. should not be overlooked as a vital part of portfolios because research indicates that all students do not express themselves best through writing. You also can learn much about your students through their illustrations. For example, you can gain an understanding of their attention to factual or fictional details; their ability to recall events in stories or articles; their understanding of characterization, mood, place, and time; their knowledge of textual and artistic media; and their ability to use various artistic devices.

◆ Collaborative Works

Projects completed in pairs or in small groups provide opportunities for students to develop their knowledge interactively. As you observe these collaborative efforts, you will be able to evaluate your students' interpersonal behaviors, discussion characteristics, problem-solving techniques, and level and quality of task completion. You can also monitor individual fulfillment of assigned tasks and roles within the group through observation or by measuring the various components of the completed activity.

◆ Workbook Pages, Quizzes, and Tests

Workbook pages are generally used to assess students' abilities to perform particular skills—similar to those found on many standardized tests. Some worksheets may provide limited information about students' knowledge of consonant and vowel sounds, punctuation, capitalization, verb tense, etc. Including some exams and quiz papers in the portfolio may also offer some insight into your students' abilities to perform in testing situations, to recall and/or apply information, and to respond with critical analysis to carefully constructed questions.

◆ Attitude Surveys

Surveys, which you generate, give you useful information when assessing and planning for your students. Attitude surveys in response to books, content subjects, topics, events, etc. will often indicate your students' likes and dislikes, opinions, and feelings.

If you administer surveys at various points during the school year, you will often see clear evidence of growth and change in attitude. (*See Sample 1 in the Appendix, page 69.*)

◆ Reading Lists and Reviews

Book lists provide you with information about the number and types of books read, the time needed to complete books of various types and length, their age-level appropriateness, your students' topical interests, and their favorite authors, illustrators, and/or book series. Many teachers also monitor their students' understanding of the books they have read by having them include book reviews in their portfolios. (*See Samples 2–4 in the Appendix, pages 70–72.*)

◆ Self-Assessment Checklists

Self-assessment checklists are a major component of most portfolio programs. Giving students established criteria and asking them to rate their performance according to the criteria helps them to be reflective about their work and the standards by which their work is measured. (*See Samples 5–7 in the Appendix, pages 73–75.*)

◆ Self-Assessment Statements

Less structured than self-assessment checklists, these statements require your students to review their knowledge or refer to a listing of criteria for particular tasks. Generally, these statements give your students a chance to focus on those criteria they think most important. Self-assessment statements can also be used in any content area because responses can be directed toward specified skills and/or information. For variety, you also could have your students dictate, tape, or write their statements.

◆ **Teacher Comments**

Your comments, whether spoken or written, are valuable components of a portfolio program, and as your students get more involved in the formulation of their portfolios, they will recognize and seek your expertise. As an evaluative measure, comparing comments over a period of time also clearly documents student growth.

◆ **Teacher Checklists**

Checklists have quickly become the most widely used method of assessment in the portfolios. With clearly defined criteria, checklists provide a very useful source of information for measuring student growth. These instruments can be used in any content area and can be developed to address particular skills and/or information. (*See Samples 8–11 in the Appendix, pages 76–79.*)

◆ **Peer Reviews**

Peer evaluations—in a group or in pairs and using dialogue, checklists, and/or statements—develop the metacognitive abilities of all students involved while also strengthening communication skills. Peer review procedures also allow you to evaluate several students simultaneously. Many teachers feel that their students actually become better critics of their own work as a result of evaluating the works of their peers.

◆ **Parental Observations and Comments**

Observation checklists and parental comments contribute to a total understanding of your students' literacy lives. Parents can provide important information about "outside" reading and study behaviors, family attitudes toward reading and writing, and the types of literacy activities that occur in the home. Involving parents in the assessment process also provides opportunities for communication and sharing about the learning process and makes them real partners in their children's education. (*See Samples 12–15 in the Appendix, pages 80–83.*)

Including Multiple Drafts

One of the greatest benefits of using portfolios is the fact that you end up with actual documentation of the growth and change in your students' abilities. That's because rather than just highlighting polished pieces of writing, portfolios include various drafts of a single work. Not only can you analyze how students have responded to your suggestions or to peer comments but you can also see how they are able to use their thinking and creative abilities to resolve any problems or issues. You can also watch throughout the year to see how certain problems are eliminated because your students have incorporated learned elements into their base of knowledge. Finally, you—and your students—can compare and contrast works from the beginning of a year with works from the end of the year to see the development of their skills over a period of time. And in an ideal world, portfolios would be passed on from year to year so that progress could be continually monitored and evaluated.

Concluding their article "Using Portfolios to Empower Student Writers," Winfield Cooper and B. J. Brown write, "We have come to believe that, when students become more conscious of the many decisions they make in order to improve their writing, when they begin to be aware of the processes they must engage in to produce effective writing, and when they finally look over a body of their work, judging it against a set of criteria they have developed and internalized, they are engaged in the kind of thinking characteristic of writers" [*English Journal*, Feb. 1992].

3 Assessing Portfolios

Assessment of what children have learned in the classroom has almost always meant testing. To assess their students' achievements, teachers traditionally use standardized tests, which are usually mandated by state education boards, and/or informal tests, which they generally devise themselves. The results of such tests, of course, provide members of school boards with information that ranks their students against national and state standards.

Critics of such testing believe, however, that these kinds of tests alone do not provide sufficient information about individual student achievement and progress. What's more, feedback from traditional tests is usually limited to percentiles or scores, and translating such statistical information into practical guidelines for classroom instruction is difficult, if not impossible.

It is curious that outside the classroom there are few places in which individuals are placed in such an unnatural testing situation. "Testing" in the workplace usually occurs within an individual's environment. For example, assessment of most clerical workers is based on their performance in the office, and factory workers are expected to meet a production quota while maintaining product quality levels. Even teachers are evaluated based on classroom observations. The list is almost endless—suggesting that there are no paper and pencil tests that provide greater evidence of one's abilities than assessment of that person's performance of an actual real-life task. And, when observations are used for assessment, they are usually made on several occasions—thereby providing an even more comprehensive picture of what a person can do and achieve with experience.

Why, then, do educators place so much importance on the "quick snapshot" provided by most paper and pencil tests? Do they believe that the ability of students to choose a correct answer from a small selection of deliberately misleading answers really indicates how much they know and how well they will be able to use that knowledge? Do test makers feel that the ability of students to fill in a blank with a presupplied vocabulary word will really demonstrate that they can use that word without specific contextual prompts? In other words, do educators really think that objective tests can actually find out what students know and can do?

Portfolios, on the other hand, offer students, parents, teachers, and administrators many opportunities for assessing students' performance and growth—without the unnatural circumstances and unnecessary pressure, cost, and time expenditure involved in formal and informal testing. What's more, most classroom teachers already know more about their students than what standardized tests can tell them. They routinely keep files on their students, collect samples of their work, and sometimes even write anecdotal records or observational logs because they know—as you know—that the information from these sources is always more meaningful in helping to assess students' abilities and to plan for classroom instruction than any data from objective tests.

Beginning the Assessment Process

Essential to the success of enlisting teachers in a portfolio assessment program is a clearly specified list of expectations concerning the composition, disposition, evaluation, and purpose of portfolios. By clearly defining the components and purposes of the portfolio assessment program, teachers are less inclined to be wary about using portfolios in their classrooms. For example, teachers need to know before they begin to implement portfolio assessment in their classrooms how much latitude they and their students will have in deciding the contents of the portfolio. Also, when teachers understand that the focus of such a program is to more effectively evaluate students, they will be less fearful that the portfolios will, in some way, be used to make judgments about the efficacy of their teaching.

Then, even before your students start to compile their portfolios, you will need to make some decisions about ways in which their portfolios will be evaluated. Some of your decisions may be based on the grading requirements of your school or on criteria suggested by members of a faculty committee or by other knowledgeable educators. One important contribution that you can make in advance of this process is to review all available professional literature, including journals, teachers' magazines, and curriculum guides for recommended materials, activities, and assessment criteria. Then, with your school committee or fellow teachers, choose those items that you feel are appropriate for your school.

Setting the Purpose

Setting the overall purpose or purposes of portfolio assessment in your classroom should be one of the first major decisions you make because so much of what else you will do depends on what you decide. As you read over some of the following basic purposes of portfolio assessment, consider which are applicable to you and your students.

◆ **To examine growth over time and purpose**

Items in the portfolio demonstrate what students have learned about a particular task over a period of time. For example, students' knowledge and use of punctuation will be clearly evidenced in their work.

◆ **To develop a sense of process**

As students return to tasks to make suggested changes, they come to understand that a finished work is the end product of a process of careful deliberation.

◆ **To create means for student self-evaluation**

Students develop criteria for judging their work by observing and internalizing standards and models presented to them.

◆ **To help students and teachers determine and set individual goals**

Since the portfolio is a record of a student's growth, it is easy to identify the student's strengths and target any weaknesses that need additional work. In this way, the portfolio helps to individualize instruction for each student.

◆ **To empower students**

As students develop a sense of ownership of their portfolios, they will take ownership of their ideas. They will recognize that knowledge is acquired as part of a participatory process and that what they learn can be utilized to express their needs and wants.

◆ **To provide real-life learning opportunities**

Items typically included in the portfolio are reflective of actual day-to-day thinking, reading, and writing tasks, and students are asked to hypothesize, analyze, and respond to ideas.

◆ **To observe growth in nondominant culture populations**

Because formalized tests are generally standardized on mainstream populations, nondominant culture students are not accounted for in norming procedures. Further, they may require additional time parameters during testing to "translate" language, relate culture phenomenon to their own cultures, compensate for physical limitations, etc. Portfolios afford opportunities to observe growth without the restrictions inherent in formalized testing situations.

◆ **To observe language development across ages and cultures**

Portfolios serve as unobtrusive and practical tracking devices for language comprehension and use because they contain items that demonstrate actual language use.

◆ **To evaluate and develop curriculum**

A continuous review of portfolios offers teachers ongoing opportunities to evaluate what their students already know, what they've learned, and what they still need to know. As a result, curriculum can be developed and revised to meet the particular needs of their students.

◆ **To determine efficacy of teaching practices**

Review of students' portfolios also sheds light on which pedagogical approaches work best with a particular class or particular students.

◆ **To facilitate faculty discussion about goals and means**

Because portfolios offer tangible evidence of what students are learning, they also provide insights into which programs and approaches work most successfully with particular populations. Information obtained from the portfolios is also helpful when discussing program direction and student needs.

◆ **To empower teachers and provide support for making changes**

Through conferencing and portfolio review, teachers come to see how directly their efforts impact on what students learn. Insights gained help teachers identify ways they can increase their impact by making any necessary changes.

Organizing Portfolios

Once you have decided on your overall purpose(s) of portfolio assessment, you and your students need to jointly zero in on the objective(s) of individual pieces that will be placed in their portfolios. For example, one objective may be to demonstrate gains in reading and writing proficiency, a growth in vocabulary, the utilization of research skills, a knowledge of available reference resources, or the ability to work collaboratively. Once these objectives are jointly established, you and your students will both share in the responsibility of fulfilling them.

As part of the assessment process, you also may find that students themselves want to create a list of objectives they'd like to work toward in completing their assignments. For example, students may decide that they want to work on punctuation or the development of a story line. They may make a list of rules for periods and commas or list the components of a story: plot, character, crisis, and resolution. After they've finished their work, they would then check off those objectives they feel they've attained. Including these evaluative measures, along with the showcased work itself, is an excellent way to provide a comprehensive assessment of your students' abilities. By including the evaluative measures, you will never run the risk of your students' portfolios simply becoming a repository for reams of paper.

Well into the assessment process, you probably will make another wonderful discovery: your students will become reflective of the processes through which they developed and evaluated their work. Once that happens, they will begin to incorporate into their work the standards they have been using as a guide to evaluation. To ensure their success, however, it will be necessary for you to provide opportunities for your students to work on building metacognitive processes. Individual teacher-student conferencing sessions, peer-peer discussions, and parent-child "homeworking" time (through the use of assignments, checklists, and shared readings) will all help to strengthen their self-reflective abilities.

Analyzing Portfolios

Once again, the purpose of the portfolio defines the type of analysis (and who will do the analyzing) of the works to be included. In some cases, checklists can provide sufficient outlines for analysis, but the evaluative criteria for self-reflective pieces, for example, may not be so concrete. Nevertheless, it is important that you always provide guidelines to everyone who will have input into the evaluative process. Peers, for instance, should never simply speculate about another student's work; they must evaluate work according to established criteria.

Keep in mind, as well, the following two major considerations when you deal with the analysis of portfolios. (1) One of the primary benefits of the portfolio assessment is the building of student reflection of cognitive processes. Therefore, all persons having input into the assessment process must be able to contribute to the students' understanding of their thinking processes. Those reviewing a portfolio, therefore, should avoid nonconstructive criticism and should, instead, provide suggestions for change that demonstrate valued criteria. All portfolio evaluators should also be available for conferencing and clarification because students cannot become reflective if they do not have opportunities to discuss their work. Initially, portfolio assessment partners are the "mirrors" by which students become reflective. (2) No one work should be considered conclusive evidence of a student's strengths or weaknesses. Every piece should be representative only of a student's abilities at the time of execution. Therefore, to draw accurate conclusions about students' abilities, you need to analyze their performance patterns over a period of time.

As you think about the how-tos of analyzing your students' portfolios, always keep in mind that students need to know in advance what will be required and expected of them. You could exhibit examples of previously completed projects so that they will have models on which to formulate their own ideas. Grading checklists and/or explanations of grades also serve to help students develop their own "expert" criteria as to what makes for a successful project.

Looking at the Practical Side

Portfolio assessment can be a natural outgrowth of what you are already doing in your classroom. Therefore, before getting started, first decide into which areas of your curriculum you want to integrate portfolio assessment. If you are currently collecting writing samples, for example, think about which stage in the writing process (brainstorming, drafting, editing) you may want your students to focus on at any particular point in the compilation of the portfolio. You can discuss and create a list of writing skills—such as note-making, outlining, researching, reviewing grammar, checking spelling—that most writers use. Then you also should develop a list of criteria that students can use as a guide in creating, understanding, and evaluating their work. Or, perhaps, you may feel your students need to develop an understanding of theme, character, or the elements of a plot in a story they have read. Jointly you and your students could draw up a reading guide that helps to identify particular features of the text and helps students monitor and evaluate their reading. Guides such as this can then be used for self-check, peer critique, and/or teacher-student conferencing. As you can see, tacking evaluative criteria onto the reading and writing your students do is one way to easily implement a portfolio assessment program into your classroom.

Another beginning step you might want to take to help your students understand the purpose and evaluate the quality of their work is to ask them to explain what they like and don't like about their writing and/or reading assignments. Open-ended questions like "Which part of your story do you like the best?" or "What didn't you like about this book?" prompt students to look reflectively at the text and to begin to respond to it. With very young children, their responses to text—whether their own text or the text of a professional author—may be tape-recorded and/or may be obtained in an interview. As students start to talk about text, they will begin to develop opinions that later will help them formulate their own evaluative criteria.

Whenever possible, you also should review your students' works with colleagues and exchange ideas and concerns. Working together like this often leads to improvements in methodology and refinements of criteria. Collaboration is also a good way to ensure objectivity in scoring.

Assessing and/or Grading

If you decide to implement portfolio assessment into your classroom, you will need to be able to answer the following questions that deal with the important issue of grades.

◆ What/Whose criteria will you use in assessing students' portfolios?

◆ How will you calculate traditional grades (A, B, C . . .) based on your students' portfolios—if at all?

◆ How will you deal with issues of subjectivity in grading?

◆ Will you incorporate portfolios into your usual testing routine or will tests become part of their portfolio collections?

◆ Will your assessment procedures supplement or replace formal and informal tests?

◆ Will tests continue to play a major role in classroom placement and/or curricular objectives, or will the tests be weighted with samples of students' work for making educational decisions?

◆ How will using portfolios impact on teachers in your students' subsequent grades or in other school districts?

While there is an occasional movement away from an emphasis on grades, the truth of the matter is that grades are still seen as a fairly accurate measure of a student's accomplishments by most of the educational establishment. Many schools still use grade point average as one factor in determining class placement purposes; it is the single most important criteria in determining class rank. College admissions offices also continue to rely heavily upon g.p.a. when making acceptance decisions. Therefore, if your school continues to use a traditional grading system, it will be necessary for you to devise a means of determining grades based on information from the portfolio—such as one of the following.

♦ Analytic holistic scoring procedures can be created for the purpose of calculating students' grades. (*For more information about alternative grading, see Chapter 6, pages 60–61.*)

♦ A listing of criteria for particular grade ranges can be established. With such a system, students would have to fulfill a percentage of the specified criteria to obtain a score within a particular range.

♦ Report cards could be redesigned to include narrative statements, narrative and grade components, and/or descriptive labels to replace traditional grades. For example, an *A* grade might have the label "Demonstrates superior ability to identify and assess important ideas in text." Labels should be more substantive and less negative than some traditionally used markers, such as "Satisfactory" and "Needs Improvement." These report cards could be designed as a checklist to include blank spaces for written remarks.

♦ Achievement reports could replace report cards or be given in addition to report cards. At the end of each traditional marking period, students and teachers could put together a listing of accomplished activities, works in progress, and designated goals. A variation of this report might even include sections in which both teacher and student discuss and evaluate the items included in each category.

♦ Parent-student-teacher portfolio conferences could take the place of report cards altogether or be used to interpret report cards according to the students' portfolios. Whether used with or in place of report cards, summary notes on each conference should be taken and included within the portfolio.

Many leading advocates of portfolio assessment initially suggested that portfolios would totally replace standardized tests (and some still do), but much of this early enthusiasm has been muted by the realities of the classroom setting, administrative concerns, and national policy. As long as traditional grades continue to maintain their stronghold on the national consciousness, adaptive techniques for scoring will have to be created. Portfolio assessment, at the least, still holds the only promise of focusing attention on criteria rather than on grades.

Portfolio Assessment vs. Standardized Testing

Portfolio Assessment	Standardized Testing
• occurs in the child's natural environment	• is an unnatural event
• provides an opportunity for student to demonstrate his/her strengths as well as weaknesses	• provides a summary of child's failures on certain tasks
• gives hands-on information to the teacher on the spot	• provides little diagnostic information
• allows the child, parent, teacher, staff to evaluate the child's strengths and weaknesses	• provides ranking information
• is ongoing, providing multiple opportunities for observation and assessment	• is a one-time "snapshot" of a student's abilities on a particular task
• assesses realistic and meaningful daily literacy tasks	• assesses artificial tasks, which may not be meaningful to the child
• invites the child to be reflective (metacognitive) about his/her work and knowledge	• asks child to provide a singular desired response
• invites the parent to be reflective of child's work and knowledge	• provides parent with essentially meaningless and often frightening numerical data
• encourages teacher-student conferencing	• forces teacher-administration conferences
• informs instruction and curriculum; places child at center of the educational process	• reinforces idea that the curriculum is the center of the educational process

---

A Word of Caution

If you are going to incorporate portfolio assessment in any way into your classroom routine, it is important that you fully understand your purpose and know what your desired goals are. This book (along with the articles and books recommended in the bibliography) provides you with a theoretical overview and practical suggestions for using portfolios. But, it is crucial that you know not only how but also why these theories, suggestions, and materials apply to your population. You will need to consider what information you do not currently have about your students, what test data is inconsistent with your classroom observations, and what educational objectives you can establish based on portfolios that you cannot make based on test score information. Knowing this information beforehand will help you to define the direction of portfolio use in your classroom and will prepare you to explain exactly why portfolios are a better measure and diagnostic tool than standardized tests.

Managing Portfolios

4

Managing portfolios is not an easy task if the job falls entirely on you. Therefore, you need to see yourself not as a collector of work samples for portfolios but rather as a coordinator. By discussing with your students the purposes and the practices of keeping portfolios, much of the responsibility for not only compiling but also evaluating their work samples will be placed where it belongs—in their hands, the hands of the portfolio owners.

Assigning Reasonable Responsibility

Whenever students feel involved in an activity, they usually will invest greater energies in doing that task well. It is not unreasonable, therefore, to give students the major responsibility of compiling and evaluating their own work. It would be unreasonable, of course, to give them such a task without telling them why they are doing it and without explaining to them how the task should be done.

Traditionally, teachers have assigned work to students with little or no explanation about the purpose of the assignment. Explanations about how the assignment was to be completed were usually abundant, but students rarely understood the purpose behind the practice. Also, they were seldom allowed to be part of the evaluation process.

In contrast, the portfolio classroom is a child-centered one. Teachers in these classrooms trust children to learn—not only from their mistakes but from their strengths as well. Because children respond to praise and recognition, they almost always will repeat whatever they did well. As a result, portfolio teachers eagerly invite students into the evaluative process. Standard procedure, therefore, includes the advance explanation of each activity and its measurement criteria. Students are then encouraged to question and express any doubts or concerns. They are also encouraged to suggest alternatives to activities, evaluation instruments, materials, etc. Always remember that students who are thinking of other ways to handle a task are thinking about the task, and if they are involved in the process, they are more likely to learn from it.

Reviewing Portfolios: How Often?

Unless time is set aside for assessing the portfolios during each school day, you will quickly begin to feel overwhelmed and frustrated with the volume of work you'll be encountering. However, reviewing every portfolio every day will never be a possibility! In fact, trying to review every portfolio too frequently will usually result in the sacrificing of quality evaluation for quantity evaluation. What's more, if there is excessive evaluation, students often become caught up in the product rather than tuned into the process.

Frequent evaluation also leaves little opportunity for reflection because students are constantly busy completing checklists or writing self-evaluative pieces. When this happens, they quickly lose energy and run out of things to say. They begin to feel that learning comes with too many strings attached and that evaluating their own work is a chore—rather than a personally satisfying task.

It is better if you develop a rotating schedule in which you can evaluate two to three portfolios each day—thereby ensuring that you will see every student's portfolio at least once during the month. The amount of time you spend on student-teacher conferences, and self-, parent-, and peer-review sessions is valuable time spent assessing your students' portfolios.

Conferencing: The Hows and Whys

You will also have to establish a revolving schedule for meeting with individual students, small groups, and the class to review and discuss the portfolios and various assessment measures. Individual conferences should be scheduled during silent reading periods, individual desk-work times, and peer-evaluation sessions. Ideally you should create a schedule that allows you to meet individually with each student at least once a month. Item placement, evaluation criteria, portfolio organization, and assessment results are all topics that can be addressed in individual conference sessions.

During conferencing, you will have repeated opportunities to establish trust and create a safe environment in which decision making is encouraged. As a result, your students will be challenged to shape change for themselves by choosing the form their portfolios will take and by deciding which works best exemplify their efforts and strengths. You should also encourage them to discuss their own observations about their growth, compare those observations with your assessments, and—with your help—devise appropriate plans for improvement and development.

The conference period, however, should not be a time to point out your students' failures and to advise them that they are "not working up to their potential." Rather, the purpose of assessment is to identify weaknesses and provide suggestions for growth. Showing students the possibilities in their work—rather than focusing on the problems—will provide them with an immediate plan of action for making changes.

During the conference period, you also will have many opportunities to do one-on-one modeling of critical thinking and decision making, and you will have many opportunities to observe your students' reasoning through the complex issues of the portfolio process. However, to avoid confusion and feelings of being over-whelmed, conferences are best limited to one or two topics at a time. Setting an agenda beforehand, based on needs identified in the port-folios, ensures a full and thoughtful discussion of the specified items.

To be sure that everyone understands and remembers what was agreed upon during each conference, both you and your students should jot down notes about your meeting when it is over. These notes can then become contracts of agreement and serve as checklists to be examined in future sessions. The notes should also be placed in the portfolio for later review. If you and your students follow this procedure, the conference itself becomes an evaluative measure and part of the portfolio's anecdotal history of developmental growth.

Involving Parents

To encourage your students' parents to become partners in this new venture, you may want to start out by sending a note home that explains a little bit about portfolio assessment and what you will be expecting their sons and daughters to do throughout the year. Also let them know that you would like them to actively participate in the formulation of their child's portfolio by giving specific responses to entries in it.

For instance, you could send home modified checklists along with clear instructions for use in working with their children. Include an expected completion date but provide ample time so that even busy parents will be able to become involved in their children's education.

Whenever possible, you also could invite parents to meet with you at school or even organize a meeting with a group of parents that will become a supportive network. At any such meetings, you should, of course, be prepared to address parents' concerns about this new and different way of assessing their children. A good idea is to have some literature available for anyone who wants more information. Including parents in the portfolio process, of course, strengthens a very important educational link among teachers, students, and parents.

Accessing Portfolios

Who should have access to portfolios? This question should have a simple answer, but it doesn't because the issue of access depends upon the purpose of a portfolio. If someone does not have a definite reason for wanting to examine a portfolio, then he or she really should not be given access to its contents. Good evaluators know what they are looking for, or they have notions of what they think they'll find. Students, in both cases, must be informed of how their portfolios will be used so that they can make judgments about any requests by others to review their work.

Certainly, in all cases, owners must have easy access to their own work. If your students know where their work is located and that they can review it whenever they want—or during scheduled times—there is increased opportunity for reflection. Of course, you also need to have access to your students' portfolios, although the frequency and purpose of such access should be clearly outlined—and perhaps even negotiated—with them at the onset of compiling the portfolios. If students feel that their teachers have too many rules or are too invasive, they will be less likely to approach the task of compilation enthusiastically.

Students may choose to invite peer review of their portfolios or allow certain sections of their portfolios to be a part of a public domain. Of course, issues of pride and privacy are very important when establishing guidelines for peer review, and sensitivity and respect for fellow students must also be built. Sometimes there is a lot of groundwork that must be laid in this area; however, teachers who model positive handling of criticism and interaction rarely have difficulties building a cooperative spirit in a classroom.

Parental review of the portfolios should also be negotiated and guidelines established from the very beginning. Students will need to know how their parents will be involved in the evaluative process and how the collected information will be used. They should never have to fear, for example, that they might be grounded because of a "bad" work sample or checklist in their portfolios.

Networking

It would be very helpful for any teachers who are newly involved in the portfolio process to establish a network with other portfolio users. Educational programs at many local colleges and universities provide a good source for locating others involved in portfolio assessment. A newsletter, the *Portfolio News*, published by the Portfolio Assessment Clearing House, is another excellent way to make connections, find support, and share ideas. (*For the address, see page 68 in the Appendix.*)

◆ 5 ◆ Benefiting from Portfolio Assessment

During the past several decades new theories have emerged that are very different from traditional views of how children learn to read and write. For many years, for instance, researchers thought that children could only learn to read and write a few monosyllabic words at a time. Children at age five were seen as blank slates onto which only little bits of information could slowly be added.

Classroom teachers today know that this long-held view of the emergent reader/writer as a blank slate is an inaccurate one. Even at very early ages children already have slates filled with information about the world in which they live. What's more, they are eager to share that information through writing and are excited about collecting new data through reading.

Multiple Benefits

Portfolios and portfolio assessment mirror the actual processes in which children are engaged as they develop their reading and writing abilities. Portfolios serve as evidence that children are learning, despite occasional departures from traditional curriculum. For example, invented spelling is somewhat less frightening to parents when a portfolio reveals that their child is beginning to adopt conventional spellings after a period of time.

Portfolios also demonstrate that children become increasingly aware of what makes a piece of work of publication quality. Initially, comments about stories children have written may center on the illustrations they've done: "I like the pictures I drew." However, later comments reveal more critical evaluation: "I liked researching the country of Brazil and drawing the map for the report."

Because portfolios document student growth and development as well as program effectiveness, you can use them with many proven educational approaches—thus multiplying the benefits of portfolio use. Following are just a few examples.

Integrated Reading and Writing Across the Curriculum

Many educators have long argued that reading and writing are inseparable processes that ought to be taught as such. Researchers point out that as children learn to read, they acquire information about the way language works in its printed form. As a result, children learn that both reading and writing are meaning-making activities. In other words, one person attempts to communicate his or her thoughts to another person, who then attempts to understand those thoughts. Children also learn that these ideas are not always clearly conveyed or easily understood. In conversation with more proficient users of the language—such as parents, older siblings, and teachers—children will often seek clarification of ideas by asking "What?" or "Why?"

When encountering print, however, readers don't have the opportunity to ask for clarification. All readers, young and old alike, must rely upon their knowledge of the world to make meaning from text. The use of this background information to interpret text points out how children do *not* learn to read and write in a vacuum. Printed matter will only contain meaning when they understand the context of the text; hence, the importance of teaching reading and writing within the curriculum, not as separate components of the curriculum.

Reading and writing are reciprocal processes; they imitate each other. When youngsters are first exposed to some of the classics of children's literature, for instance, they quickly come to believe that most stories begin with "Once upon a time. . . ." As children move on to read different kinds of texts, they begin to recognize the different styles of writing. Journalistic pieces are written differently from works of fiction and from pieces of poetry. As a result, in most cases adept readers become adept writers and are, at the least, able to dabble in expressing themselves in alternate writing styles.

Portfolios, which are continued across extended periods of time and/or grade levels, not only monitor childrens' development as writers by showing their attempts and abilities at using different writing styles but also present evidence of the students' growth as readers by reflecting exposure to works of different genre and style. Portfolios also easily demonstrate the strengths of a curriculum that integrates reading and writing across all content areas.

The Writing Process

Lucy Caulkins, author of *The Art of Teaching Writing*, notes, "When I went to school, writing was rarely taught; rather, it was assigned and then corrected. . . . [The teachers'] emphasis was on final products, not on the processes that produced them" (p. 13). For many students, the red pen is one of the most dreaded of classroom objects. Writing has frequently been reduced to an exercise in grammar rather than an opportunity to make meaningful statements or pass on important information. While grammar certainly is important in the finished product, making meaning must be the primary object of all expression.

In recent years the process approach to writing has gained tremendous favor throughout the nation as an excellent way to generate meaningful and grammatically correct written text. There are basically three stages central to this approach. The first is the prewriting stage. At this point, students organize their thoughts about a topic by brainstorming ideas, researching relevant materials, making webs or charts that outline the intent of their work, and by interviewing persons who will provide useful information.

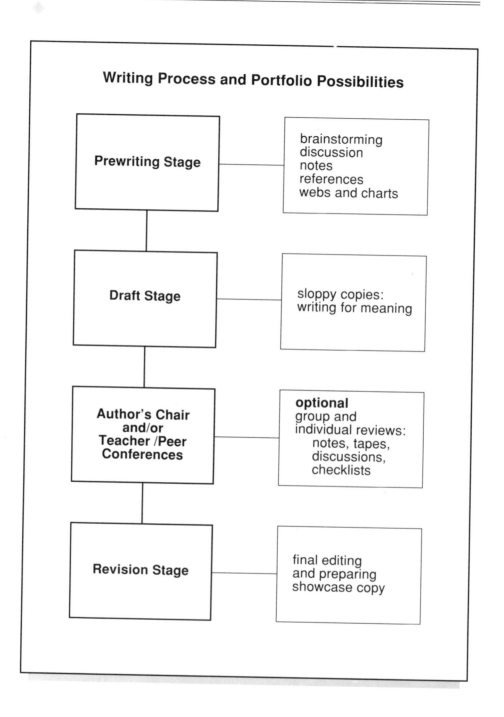

Writing Process and Portfolio Possibilities

Prewriting Stage	brainstorming discussion notes references webs and charts
Draft Stage	sloppy copies: writing for meaning
Author's Chair and/or Teacher /Peer Conferences	**optional** group and individual reviews: notes, tapes, discussions, checklists
Revision Stage	final editing and preparing showcase copy

The second stage of the writing process is often referred to as the "sloppy copy stage" or the drafting stage. At this point, students jot down their ideas without concern for spelling, grammar, and handwriting. In this freewriting stage, they focus on writing for meaning, concentrating on getting their ideas down and conveying their thoughts to an audience.

During this stage, many teachers like to incorporate a procedure known as the Author's Chair [Graves and Hansen, 1983]. After completing a draft copy, students come together to critique one another's work. Generally, one student sits in a special "author's chair" and describes his/her own questions and concerns about the written piece. The listeners offer suggestions and ask questions that enable the author to revise the piece to meet the needs of the audience.

The final, essential stage of the writing process approach is the revision and editing stage. Before handing in their papers, students revise their work for meaning and proofread and edit it for spelling and grammar mistakes. This may also be done individually, or it can be done with students working in pairs, in groups, and/or in conference with the teacher. Most teachers then have their students "publish" their final papers by hanging them on a bulletin board, reading them aloud, or any other number of possibilities that allow their students to share their finished work with others.

The portfolio serves as an excellent vehicle for providing examples of students' work at the various stages of the writing process. For example, research notes and personal interviews from the prewriting stage shed light on how students went about collecting and utilizing information. Annotated (underlined, highlighted, or marginally notated) articles or essays also provide data on which and how many reference sources students selected, on what ideas in the text they found most important, and how well they were able to analyze and summarize critical ideas in the text.

Contrasting sloppy copies with later sloppy copies and/or the final copy also demonstrates students' growth with the topic, style of writing, and use of conventional spelling and grammar. Reading their notes, comments, and suggestions made in peer conferences or teacher conferences and examining changes based on those ideas also provide insight into not only how effectively students utilize criticism to clarify and correct their work but also how well they respond to criticism. Finally, reviewing any included self-checklists and peer checklists (for style, grammar, spelling, etc.) may yield additional information about how much students have learned and applied to their work.

No standardized test has yet been able to provide classroom teachers with so much important information about how their students generate, research, edit, and discuss their ideas. Portfolios are themselves works in process that provide assessment of other works in process.

Whole Language

In recent years, whole language classrooms have begun to replace the traditional classroom because an emphasis on the curriculum has been replaced by an emphasis on the child. The role of the teacher has changed from that of "keeper" of the knowledge to that of "facilitator" of learning experiences. Kenneth Goodman (1986), in his book *What's Whole in Whole Language?*, says that "Whole language is an attempt to get back to basics in the real sense of that word—to set aside basals, workbooks, and tests, and to return to inviting kids to learn to read and write by reading and writing real stuff" (p. 38). When students construct meaning in their reading and writing activities, they learn about the language by actually using it.

The whole language classroom is one in which learning is multidimensional rather than segmented and arbitrarily sequenced. Skills are learned as children need them, not when curriculum creators say they should be learned, and skills are learned, not taught, within a meaningful and relevant context. Phonics, spelling, and punctuation, for instance, are modeled in good children's literature and by the classroom teacher, who often thinks aloud to demonstrate the processes involved in making meaning. Students are encouraged to take risks for themselves in reading and writing by making predictions about text, debating and selecting particular ideas, and using their knowledge about how language works to spell and choose grammatical forms. What is most important to understand about whole language is that it is not an approach but a philosophy that believes that children learn best when they learn naturally—when they direct the course of their own learning.

Portfolios and portfolio assessment incorporate the philosophy that learning—and the evaluation of that learning—must occur naturally. Portfolios allow students to make decisions about which works to showcase and how to critically evaluate them. Therefore, they

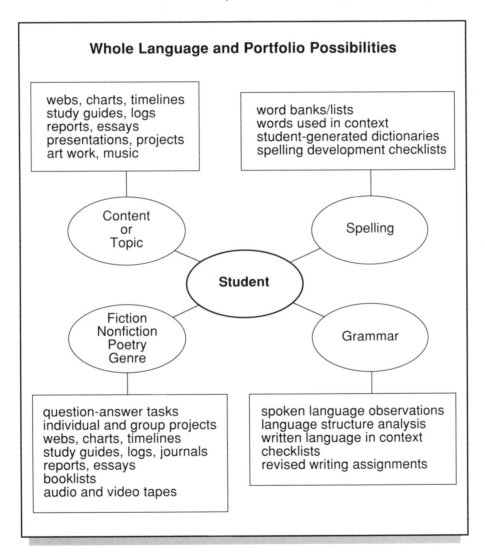

Whole Language and Portfolio Possibilities

webs, charts, timelines
study guides, logs
reports, essays
presentations, projects
art work, music

word banks/lists
words used in context
student-generated dictionaries
spelling development checklists

Content
or
Topic

Spelling

Student

Fiction
Nonfiction
Poetry
Genre

Grammar

question-answer tasks
individual and group projects
webs, charts, timelines
study guides, logs, journals
reports, essays
booklists
audio and video tapes

spoken language observations
language structure analysis
written language in context
checklists
revised writing assignments

direct the course of the evaluation of their learning. Because portfolio assessment is not arbitrarily imposed or created, it becomes unobtrusive and reality based. What's more, portfolios naturally trace and evaluate students' learning throughout the school year and, if used across all grade levels, throughout their academic lives.

Portfolios as Acts of Metacognition

One term that is bandied about quite frequently in reading circles these days is *metacognition*, or *metacomprehension*. If you are *metacognitive*, you are reflective about your thinking processes. In other words, you are able to understand why you think and act in a particular manner. Most people, for instance, do not stop reading a very interesting book when they come to a word they don't recognize. Instead of stopping to look up the word in the dictionary, they put into action a series of cognitive processes to help them determine the meaning of the word. For example, they will scan the preceding and following text for clues about the word's meaning, make some assumptions about the meaning of the word, and narrow down the assumptions until they decide upon a definition that seems to fit. Then they will monitor the subsequent paragraphs to make sure the definition continues to work. All of this is done, of course, in a matter of seconds! If someone were to ask them why they didn't stop to look the word up in the dictionary, they probably would answer with some confidence that they knew they could probably figure out the meaning of the word from its context.

Proficient readers make other decisions about what processes they will engage in as they read. For example, they set a purpose for their reading; a work of fiction may be read for fun, whereas a textbook may be read to locate particular information. They also make decisions about what they read; halfway through the murder mystery, they may have concluded that the butler didn't do it after all. As they read, they also evaluate the text and draw conclusions: "This story was so unbelievable!" Less proficient readers don't utilize these processes as frequently, and some troubled readers may even be unaware that they can interact with a text. Often, these readers simply push through a text to get finished with it—rather than to make meaning from it.

Because portfolios invite reflection, they provide a means for readers to take what they are doing mentally and to put it into some kind of tangible form. Portfolios give their owners opportunities to evaluate what they've read or written and to make decisions about what was important to them in the text. In other words, portfolios give their owners a chance to be metacognitive about the kinds of things they did as they read the text. If reading is a series of metacognitive acts, then assembling the portfolio is the proof of those acts.

Metacognitive readers . . .

Before Reading
- Review their background knowledge on the subject.
- Identify a purpose for reading.
- Establish a comfortable/suitable reading environment.

During Reading
- Attend to the reading task.
- Monitor their reading comprehension routinely and automatically.
- Use reading strategies to make meaning as they go.
- Stop, reread, and employ particular strategies when meaning is unclear.

After Reading
- Decide if they met their purpose for reading.
- Evaluate their understanding of what was read.
- Summarize ideas—on paper and/or in their heads.
- Seek additional information, if necessary.
- Connect information to other knowledge.

Nonmainstream Students

Portfolio assessment provides a clear picture of the abilities and thought processes of student populations not well served by traditional standardized testing. Students whose native language is not the native language of the school community, or who are from populations that are other than that of the dominant culture, often encounter difficulty in performing within test makers' specified ranges of normed scores. As a result, cultural bias has affected the outcomes of many tests. All too often, students from populations viewed as *minority*—even when the students of these various cultures are actually in the *majority*—are asked questions that are not relevant to their experience or their environments. In many cases, these students do not fail the test; it is the test that fails them. Such students are not *culturally deprived* as some educators have suggested, but rather they are *other culture-enriched*.

Student-created portfolios provide insights into the richness of their dominant cultures and offer data on their cognitive processes. Because portfolios encourage reflection of all cultures, they demonstrate the growth of the portfolio owners—regardless of their cultural heritage. What's more, the portfolios of other-culture-enriched students serve to enhance, educate, and inform all of the other members of the classroom.

All too often, students who are labeled *disabled* or *disadvantaged* and are placed in special educational or enrichment programs are so designated because the evaluative criteria on which their classifications are based focused on the students' weaknesses rather than on their strengths and abilities. Because students who are perceived as deficient rarely are given opportunities to demonstrate what they can do, they often become passive recipients of information rather than active participants in the learning process. Unfortunately they then become handicapped more by their labels and by their remedial programs than by any real or actual weaknesses.

The use of portfolios, on the other hand, allows differently abled students to state and affirm what they have learned and to make judgments about their learning—processes no less important to non-mainstream students than to mainstream students. By focusing on their strengths rather than on their weaknesses, students are empowered by what they have learned. They are also able to connect the information they've amassed and apply it meaningfully to their own life situations. As a result, they no longer have to feel limited by what they don't know, but they are able to take risks based on the validation of what they do know. In other words, portfolios allow these students, who are all too often disenfranchised from the academic community, to demonstrate their active and eager involvement in their educational lives.

6 Dealing with Possible Portfolio Problems

So far this book has dealt with the many advantages and benefits of portfolio assessment, but no educational program or system is entirely free of problems—especially when they are administered by teachers with differing experiences and insights and are administered to children of all ages and backgrounds.

Problems and Solutions

Many of the school districts that plunged early and eagerly into using portfolios have had some time now to reflect upon what they are doing with the mountains of information they've collected. They have also begun to confront and deal with some of the problems inherent in a portfolio assessment program.

Validity of Portfolio Assessment

The greatest problem for portfolio evaluators is convincing some members of the educational community that portfolios are valid measures of what students know. *Validity* is a term researchers use to indicate that an instrument or experiment has measured what the experimenter wanted to measure. For some in education, the validity of portfolio assessment is questionable because it does not provide the same normalized statistics that standardized tests offer. But, even among educators, there can be no question that portfolios offer a valid measure of the types of learning tasks most encountered in life.

The schools that have succeeded in establishing validity have made extraordinary attempts to educate the community. Since portfolio assessment ultimately calls into question some long-held notions of how students should be graded, many schools and/or districts have recognized how essential an effective information outreach program is to the success of a portfolio-based approach. Parent-teacher organization meetings, community presentations with informed guest speakers, workshops, and roundtable discussions have all helped portfolio assessment gain acceptance by parents, local politicians, and business leaders.

Criteria Selection

Selecting criteria for evaluating proficiency can be a difficult task. Because the selection process can be somewhat arbitrary, many school districts have put together faculty committees (often with administrative and parental input) to define criteria and to create checklists and materials that can be used by both teachers and students for evaluating work. By convening a group of educators from within the school, administrators can not only encourage district-wide adoption of the portfolio program but also can establish standard criteria.

The job of the faculty committee, however, is never over once it has begun. Many school districts continue to convene their committees periodically because checklists and other materials developed at one point in the portfolio process may not meet the assessment needs or fit the changing educational philosophy of the school at a later point. Furthermore, teachers soon recognize which checklists do not accurately measure the qualities the committee had originally hoped they would. In addition, new criteria should be continually added to the assessment process as the students and the program grow.

Teacher Assessment

For most teachers, diagnosing problems, providing instruction, and selecting appropriate materials are a routine part of their daily teaching experience. Still, some teachers are hesitant to make hard and fast evaluations about student performance in the absence of clearly specified criteria. When this happens, those same teachers too often discount what they know about their students and yield their assessment decisions to the statisticians who compile the norms charts that come with standardized tests. Therefore, teachers themselves must be educated to understand that portfolio assessment can be an empowering agent because it guarantees teachers the opportunity to use their professional and personal expertise to make assessments and to develop a plan of educational intervention for their students.

Assessment Objectivity

Even with the use of checklists and criteria outlines, many teachers will still feel uncomfortable assessing students without the ease and security of a 100-point system. As a result, checklists have been devised that assign each criteria a certain amount or a range of points. Teachers can then calculate a number grade or percentage based on the number of criteria satisfied. This method is often referred to as analytic holistic scoring [Cooper, 1977].

Another method for assessing what students have learned and for obtaining a numerical score is the Descriptive Marking Scale. This measure provides teachers with a set of objectives and scoring criteria for each objective. In addition, a range of scores for each item is provided. Classroom teachers select the appropriate criteria and assign a score for each objective. A grade can then be determined by calculating a percentage based on the total of range scores.

To maintain objectivity and uphold integrity in assessing student work, many school districts arrange for teams of teachers to assess portfolios and work samples. Many research studies have demonstrated that, with sufficient training and similar educational philosophy, there is high reliability among raters using holistic evaluation procedures.

Essay Grade Checklist

Student _____

Essay Title _____

1. The essay focuses on a particular subject.

   Range Score: 0 ❯ 10 points.   Points: _____

2. The essay has appropriate beginning, middle, and ending sections.

   Range Score: 0 ❯ 10 points.   Points: _____

3. The sequence of events is logical.

   Range Score: 0 ❯ 10 points.   Points: _____

4. The essay maintains its voice (first person or third person).

   Range Score: 0 ❯ 10 points.   Points: _____

5. Verb tense and agreement are appropriately used.

   Range Score: 0 ❯ 10 points.   Points: _____

6. The essay is written using complete sentences.

   Range Score: 0 ❯ 10 points.   Points: _____

7. The essay contains appropriate descriptive language.

   Range Score: 0 ❯ 10 points.   Points: _____

8. The essay is correctly punctuated.

   Range Score: 0 ❯ 10 points.   Points: _____

9. The essay uses rules of capitalization.

   Range Score: 0 ❯ 10 points.   Points: _____

10. The essay has been proofread for spelling errors.

   Range Score: 0 ❯ 10 points.   Points: _____

   Total points for the essay: _____

Essay Grade Checklist

Student _____

Essay Title _____

1. The essay focuses on a particular subject.   _____

　　0=lack of focus

　　1=minimal focus

　　2=moderate focus

　　3=maintains focus

2. The essay has appropriate beginning, middle, and ending sections. _____

　　0=lacks components of essay

　　1=contains one component

　　2=contains two components

　　3=contains all three components

3. The sequence of events is logical.   _____

　　0=lack of sequence

　　1=minimal sequencing

　　2=moderate sequencing

　　3=maintains sequencing throughout

4. The essay maintains its voice (first person or third person). _____

　　0=lacks consistent voice

　　1=maintains consistent voice

5. Verb tense and agreement are appropriately used.   _____

　　0=verb tense and agreement are generally incorrectly used

　　1=minimal use of correct verb tense and agreement

　　2=some use of correct verb tense and agreement

　　3=consistent use of correct verb tense and agreement

Total points achieved:　_____

Total possible:　13

Percentage Score:　_____

Student Self-Assessment

Initially, it will be difficult for students to assess themselves. They may not be used to evaluating their work simply because schools have traditionally not asked them to make judgments about what they've done. However, a basic premise of portfolio assessment is that the student independently develops the expertise to use a "mental red pen" for meaning making, correction, and editing purposes. The teacher probably will have to model self-evaluation techniques and/or demonstrate the use of checklists and criteria guides in the beginning, but students will soon internalize and apply these standards to their work. Then as they become metacognitive readers and writers, the "mental red pen" is no longer needed.

Parental Assessment

Some schools do not recognize the importance of parental involvement in the portfolio process. Parents should be asked to help students select pieces of work to be included in the portfolio, reflect upon their own thoughts about particular samples, and complete checklists that offer other perspectives of reading and writing growth. They might also participate in the evaluation process by relating observations of their children's literacy behaviors at home, thereby providing a view of students that teachers rarely get to see. Involving parents not only increases understanding of the aims of the portfolio program and garners support for it; such involvement also gives parents a fuller understanding of classroom activity and, in turn, they become more sensitive to the many ways in which their children learn. Such parents are also less likely to exert excessive pressure on or become critical of their children (and teachers, administrations, programs, curricula, etc.) when they are directly involved in their children's education.

Any attempts to involve parents without adequately explaining the purpose of portfolio assessment and children's learning processes, however, may cause numerous problems. Sending home a note with each assignment that describes the nature and purpose of the assignment often helps parents understand what their children have been asked to do. Guidelines, which ask for responses to specific criteria regarding observations and questions, limit and clarify the role of the parents as partners in the portfolio process.

Portfolio Mandates

If portfolio assessment is truly going to work, then it must have administrative support. However, in some school districts portfolio assessment is being mandated. Teachers are being told that they are to begin compiling work folders with checklists and student self-reflection pieces. They are also often told how many pieces of work and the types of work that should be included in the folders, how often pieces should be placed within, and how frequently students and parents should have access to the portfolios. Such an approach to implementing portfolios runs counter to all of the original goals of portfolio use.

If portfolio assessment is going to live up to its promise, then it is not enough for teachers simply to mindlessly follow a set of instructions. They must understand the philosophical thinking behind portfolio use, and they must be free to work portfolios into the routines of their classrooms. They also must have the latitude to allow their students to make decisions about the contents and analysis of portfolios.

On the other hand, other school administrators are approaching implementation of portfolio assessment by involving teachers right from the start. They reason that teachers engaged in the process of portfolio assessment will seek out and create opportunities for sharing and reflecting with others involved in the process. Then together they can refine objectives and evaluative criteria. By sharing ideas of what works and what doesn't work, teachers move toward a clearer definition of purpose, and in the process they become more effective teachers.

Some administrators are also realizing that in order to implement portfolio assessment so that it can be a meaningful part of their overall educational programs, additional funding is needed for faculty training and development, materials, parent workshops, information programs, etc. Portfolio assessment cannot succeed in school districts where it is being mandated without allocating sufficient funding for necessary resources and training.

Portfolio Ownership

In whose possession portfolios ultimately end up is a concern that needs to be adequately addressed. When a community undertakes a portfolio assessment program on a district-wide basis, portfolios can be passed on from grade level to grade level and from school to school with few problems. The required contents and evaluative procedures will be essentially the same, and the teachers will either informally acquire a background or receive training in the interpretation of the portfolios. Finally, just as school records are ultimately housed in a particular location, the portfolios can be stored along with the students' permanent K–12 files. Then, as students move on to postsecondary education, colleges and universities may be informed that the portfolios are available for viewing, provided that the students authorize release of the records to interested placement offices.

For schools in which only a handful of teachers are implementing a portfolio program, the final disposition of the portfolio could become a problem. Some teachers ask their students if they want to take the portfolios home with them at the end of the school year, and others divide the contents into two separate folders, one of which is kept with the students' permanent records. However, if the portfolio is the only assessment device used to make grading and/or placement decisions, it would probably be prudent to file the portfolio securely away. Should questions or controversies about any student's performance arise, his or her portfolio will be readily available for review and reevaluation.

Scientific Evidence

At a recent national conference of reading researchers, two frequently asked questions were "But how do we know portfolios work?" and "What are we really learning about students from their portfolios?" The plain fact at this time is that educators and researchers have not done enough experimental studies to show statistically that portfolios do work. Empirically, teachers can see that students who use portfolios are more involved in their learning. Portfolio teachers also feel that they are more in touch with their students' needs, and their students seem more willing to talk about things they don't understand. But, even from within the ranks of educators, there are those who doubt the effectiveness of portfolios. Some teachers think they are learning more about their students, even though many feel they probably could have come to the same conclusions without the portfolios. A few teachers even believe that portfolios are only helpful to other, less experienced teachers, but they don't feel a need to use portfolios themselves.

So far, no conclusive scientific evidence has been forthcoming to suggest that portfolios are an effective means of improving learning or a better alternative to standardized testing, and there is little research to indicate that good teachers learn anything new from portfolios. Some teachers have even suggested that portfolio use takes away from instructional time. With so many of these issues unexamined and so many questions unanswered, why should teachers, administrators, and school districts unhesitatingly plunge into portfolio assessment?

Obviously, there is something to what teachers think, feel, and believe about the effectiveness of portfolio use. Because teachers are the only constant observers of their students, their conclusions about the portfolio process cannot be discounted. Neither can the evidence that is amassed in the portfolios themselves be discounted. Just as a jury examines all of the exhibits in a trial to reach a verdict, portfolio teachers can readily point to conclusive evidence of students' process and product. Standardized testing can only offer a product—with no hint of how students produced the product—but portfolios can and do show the process as well.

Furthermore, any approach that involves students in their educations and that stimulates and excites them to evaluate themselves and build expertise is certainly worth the effort. A program that invites parents to become partners in learning is also definitely cause for celebration and unreserved support. In the final analysis, portfolio assessment creates a participation in learning and a form of evaluation that formalized tests have totally excluded. In her article in the *English Journal*, Margie Krest shares her own personal evaluation of portfolio use. She writes, "Though students sometimes complain because they must do a lot of writing and realize, as writers know, that writing is often hard work, their pride and confidence in themselves and their writing also increase. Years ago I had to beg students not to throw away their graded papers into the trash. Now I have to beg students to let me 'borrow' their portfolios to photocopy samples" [Feb. 1990].

Appendix

Help and Support

1. The *FairTest Examiner* is a quarterly newsletter published by the National Center for Fair & Open Testing. Memberships, which include a free subscription to the *FairTest Examiner*, can be obtained by making a contribution to this alternative testing organization. At the time of this writing, an Associate membership was available for $30.00 annually and may be purchased by sending a check made out to *FairTest* at the address provided below. Persons interested in obtaining more information about the National Center for Fair & Open Testing and/or other membership options may call (617)864-4810 or fax (617)497-2224.

> FairTest
> 342 Broadway
> Cambridge, MA 02139

2. The *Juneau School District Language Arts Portfolio Handbook* is an excellent source of materials and suggested procedures for $10.00 (at the time of this writing). To order the book or get further information, contact the Curriculum Office of the Juneau School District at (907)789-6387 or fax (907)789-4488 or write to the address provided below.

> Portfolio Handbook
> Curriculum Office
> Juneau School District
> 10014 Crazy Horse Drive
> Juneau, AK 99801

3. The *Portfolio Assessment Newsletter* is published three times a year by the Northwest Evaluation Association. Subscriptions can be obtained by sending a check--made payable to the Northwest Evaluation Association--to the address provided below. At the time of this writing, a subscription was available for $25.00 annually. Persons interested in obtaining more information about the Northwest Evaluation Association may call Dr. Allan Olson at (503)624-1951.

> Portfolio Assessment Newsletter
> 5 Centerpointe Drive, Suite 100
> Lake Oswego, OR 97035

4. *Portfolio News* is a quarterly newsletter published by the Portfolio Assessment Clearing House. Subscriptions are available for $25.00 annually (at the time of this writing) and may be purchased by sending a check made out to *Portfolio News* at the address provided below. Additional information may be obtained by contacting Dr. Donald Kemp at the San Dieguito Union High School District, (617)753-6491.

> Portfolio News: Subscriptions
> c/o San Dieguito Union High School District
> 710 Encinitas Boulevard
> Encinitas, CA 92024

Portfolio Samples

Note to Readers: The samples compiled in this appendix are just that—samples—and they are only meant to be a guide or a suggestion for formulating your own. You undoubtedly will have to alter them to meet the particular expectations of your students (their ages and abilities) and your school district.

Student Attitude Survey About Reading

Name _____ Date _____

Directions: Carefully read each statement. Then for each one,
mark a *T* for True or an *F* for False.

1. _____ I hate to read.

2. _____ After I finish a story, I like to write down my thoughts and ideas about it in my response journal.

3. _____ I'm afraid of reading aloud.

4. _____ I like reading quietly to myself.

5. _____ Sometimes I can't answer questions about a story very well because I can't remember everything about it.

6. _____ When I finish a book, I feel very proud.

7. _____ Sometimes I choose to read a book just by its cover.

8. _____ Writing two questions about what I don't understand about my reading assignment helps me to understand it better.

9. _____ Sometimes I fall behind in my reading assignments because I get bored.

10. _____ When I come across a word I don't know, I just skip it.

11. _____ Keeping a reading log is a waste of time.

12. _____ When I like a book, I try to find other books by the same author so I can read them, too.

13. _____ Sometimes I will read a book that a classmate recommends.

14. _____ I enjoy having my teacher read aloud books in class.

15. _____ I won't even try to read a book if the print is too small.

16. _____ I think 30 minutes is too long to read all at one time.

17. _____ I am aware that authors have different styles.

18. _____ I like reading aloud because I'm proud of how well I read.

19. _____ I prefer reading in a group with children who read at the same speed as I do.

20. _____ I like telling my classmates about a book I enjoyed reading.

Additional Comments: _____

_____

Student Reading Record

Name _____ School Year _____

Book Title	Author	Dates	
		Started	Finished

Directions: After reading each book, students may dictate information to you or complete the review sheet independently.

Student Book Review Sheet
(For Younger Students)

Name _____ Date _____ Grade _____

Title of Book _____

Author _____

Illustrator _____

How did you like the book? Circle your answer.

How did you like the drawings? Circle your answer.

Would you read the book again? Circle your answer.

What did you like most about this book? _____

_____

What did you like least about this book? _____

_____

Student Book Review Sheet
(For Older Students)

Name _____ Date _____ Grade _____

Title of Book _____

Author _____

Illustrator _____

Number of pages _____

1. Why did you choose this book to read? _____

_____

_____

2. Write a summary of the book. _____

_____

_____

_____

3. Explain what you liked most about this book. _____

_____

_____

4. In your opinion, how could this book have been better? _____

_____

_____

5. Explain why you would or would not recommend this book to a classmate.

_____

_____

Directions: At the beginning of the year, let the members of your class brainstorm a list of the things they would like to learn during the year. Then have each student select from the list all the items he/she would like to include on individual lists. Each list should then be placed in each student's portfolio until the spring. At that time you should have individual conferences with your students to discuss the items they selected and any specific signs of growth in those areas. After their conferences, the students should fill in the second section of this sheet.

Student Self-Reflection Activity Sheet

Name _____ Grade _____

Today's date _____

These are some things I would like to learn this year.

_____

_____

_____

_____

_____

_____

Today's date _____

These are some things I have learned this year.

_____

_____

_____

_____

_____

_____

Student-Teacher Conferencing Checklist
(Writing Guidelines for Young Children)

Student's Name _____ Date _____ Grade _____

When writing in my journal, I can do the following:

_____ I wrote about something I am interested in.

_____ I wrote a story about real people, places, and things.

_____ I wrote a make-believe story.

_____ I started at the top of the page.

_____ I wrote from left to right.

_____ I drew pictures to go along with my story.

_____ I used both capital letters and small letters.

_____ I left spaces between all of the words.

_____ I put a period or an exclamation mark at the end of every sentence.

_____ I put a question mark at the end of each question.

_____ I started each sentence with a capital letter.

_____ I made the people in my story talk.

_____ I put quotation marks around the words of the people in my story.

_____ I tried to use some new words in my story.

Others things I did when I wrote my story are

_____

_____

_____

_____

Directions: Hand these checklists out to students who want to become better readers. You also may want to send a copy of this checklist home to their parents.

Metacognitive Strategies Checklist

Name _____   Date _____

If you want to become a better reader,

Think about your book before you start to read it.

_____   Who is the author and illustrator of this book?

_____   What predictions can I make about this book based on the illustrations and what I know about the author?

_____   Why do I think the author wrote this book?

_____   Why do I want to read this book?

Think about what you're reading as you read your book.

_____   Is what I am reading making sense?

_____   Can I clearly picture what I'm reading in my mind?

_____   Do I feel I personally know the characters in this book?

_____   Where does this story take place?

_____   Do I stop and reread anything I don't understand?

_____   Do I understand the most important words?

Think back on what you have read when you're finished reading.

_____   Were my predictions about the book correct?

_____   What clues did I find throughout the book that helped me to draw some conclusions about this book?

_____   What opinions do I have about this book?

Teacher Checklist for Students' Attitude Toward Reading

Student's Name _____ Date _____ Grade _____

Criteria

1. Independently uses the classroom library.
2. Independently uses the school library.
3. Personally owns books and magazines at home.
4. Willingly shares with others any outside reading.
5. Talks to classmates about books and reading.
6. Seems to have one or more favorite authors.
7. Seeks out additional reading on subjects of personal interest.
8. Reads for enjoyment.
9. Will choose reading when there is a choice of activities.
10. Seems to be able to apply ideas from reading to his/her life.
11. Takes part in the classroom book club.
12. Takes part in the book exchange club.
13. Parents report that he/she reads independently at home.
14. Is able to answer questions correctly about reading assignments.
15. Enjoys reading books of different genre.

	Seldom	Sometimes	Often
Oct.			
Feb.			
May			

	Main Interest	Favorite Author	Favorite Book
Oct.			
Feb.			
May			

Teacher's Signature _____

Teacher Checklist for Students' Ability to Retell a Story

Student's Name _____ Date _____ Grade _____

Title and Author of Book _____

	Minimum	Moderate	Extensive
1. Includes information directly in the text.			
2. Includes inferred information in the text.			
3. Includes what is most important.			
4. Includes a summary or a generalization.			
5. Includes connections to the reader's life.			
6. Includes an attachment to reading (likes or dislikes).			
7. Recognizes the author's organization and audience.			
8. Asks additional questions.			

Teacher Checklist for Students' Ability to Retell a Story

Student's Name _____ Date _____ Grade _____

Title/Topic of Writing _____

This piece of writing shows	Midyear	End of year
1. the choice of a broad topic.		
2. the use of description, feelings, and dialogue to develop ideas and events.		
3. the choice of an interesting title that includes the main idea.		
4. a clear beginning, middle, and end that is developed chronologically.		
5. an effort to divide long narratives into cohesive chapters.		
6. a beginning that reflects classical literature.		
7. the use of capital letters at the beginning of sentences and with names.		
8. the use of invented spelling that reflects standard spelling patterns.		
9. the use of correct spelling for at least 80–90% of the words.		
10. little or no inclusion of mechanical errors that interfered with understanding.		
Overall Score		

Scores: 4 = most often; 3 = frequently; 2 = occasionally; 1 = never

Comments: _____

_____

Directions: A checklist such as this should be given to the students at the beginning of the year so that they understand what is expected of them. Then, the same checklist should be used at the end of the year as part of the portfolio's evaluation process.

Portfolio Checklist
(For Language Arts Class Only)

Name _____ Date _____

By the end of the year, your portfolio must contain the original copies of the following items.

_____ **Student Assessment Letter(s)**

(You can have your students write one per quarter or just one at the end of the year to accompany the final evaluation of the portfolio.)

This letter, directed to the reader of the portfolio, explains the rationale for the selection of the works and a self-assessment of the works.

_____ **Reading Log and Book Reviews**

(The number of book reviews will depend on the grade level.)

The reading log should be assessed on not only how many books a student read but also on the student's development as a reader—based on the books that were chosen.

_____ **Reading Attitude Survey**

(One should be completed at the beginning of the year and then compared to the same survey given at the end of the year.)

You may want to conduct the end-of-the-year survey orally so that you can better explore any change in attitude over the year.

_____ **Writing Samples**

(The number should be determined by grade level and ability.)

You can specify certain samples that you want included—such as a persuasive essay, a short story, a poem, and a short report. However, you also should let your students include several pieces of which they are most proud.

Parent Information Letter
(To Be Sent Home at the Beginning of the Year)

Date _____

Dear _____*Parents' names*_____ ,

   This year your child will be participating in an exciting new program.

_____*Child's name*_____ will be putting together a collection of his/her

work. I will use this portfolio of work samples to help determine all of your

child's strengths and any weaknesses in order to plan appropriate

classwork for him/her.

   Throughout the school year, I will ask you to review the portfolio and

share with me your comments and observations about your child's work. It

is my hope that together we will be able to help _____*Child's name*_____

grow in many new and exciting ways.

   Please call me if you have any questions or if you would like to come

into the school for a conference about portfolio assessment. I am looking

forward to working closely with you, and I can assure you that this will be an

exceptional year for all of us.

Sincerely,

_____*Teacher's name*_____

Parent Checklist for Language Skills
(For Grades 2–3)

Child's Name _____ Date _____ Grade _____

Because the teacher-student-parent link is so important to your child's education, please take the time to fill out the following checklist regarding your child's language skills. If you have time, please jot down some comments as well. Sometimes they can be extremely helpful.

My child	Usually	Some-times	Rarely	Comments
1. talks easily with friends and adults.				
2. listens carefully and responds appropriately.				
3. can follow directions that have several steps.				
4. looks forward to being read to.				
5. likes to read independently.				
6. tries to read unfamiliar words by using: meaning.				
picture clues.				
letter/sound connections.				
7. can retell a story in his/her own words.				
8. independently checks out books from a library.				
9. independently writes fiction.				
10. independently writes nonfiction.				

My child really enjoys: _____

_____

_____

Parent Checklist for Home Reading
(For Young Children)

Date _____

Dear _____*Parents' names*_____ ,

    Here is a book that _____*Child's name*_____ chose from the library today. Please take this wonderful opportunity to share this book with him/her. When you are finished, have your child return the book and this form to me so that I will be able to share this event with both of you.

Book's Title _____

Check where appropriate:

_____ I read this book to my child.

_____ My child and I read the book together.

_____ I wanted to read the book with my child, but I couldn't find enough time.

My child read the book to me by

_____ using the pictures to retell the story.

_____ using memorized words from the book.

_____ retelling the story in his/her own words.

_____ reading the words in the story.

_____ My child read the book to other members of the family.

Additional Comments: _____

_____

_____

A Family Member's Signature _____

Parent Information Sheet

Dear _____ *Parents' names* _____ ,

Following are a few guidelines that you can use to help your child become a better reader. Your reinforcement at home of what we are doing in the classroom will not only make your child a better reader but will also help to develop a life long love of reading in him/her.

Thanks for your help.

_____ *Teacher's name* _____

Before Reading:

1. Read the title and author.
2. Ask your child why he/she chose that particular book.
3. Look through all the pictures.
4. As the two of you are looking through the pictures, make guesses about what might happen in the story.

During Reading:

1. Read the story or have your child read it to you.
2. Stop and talk from time to time about the guesses you two made and how they are the same or different from what is actually happening in the story.

After Reading:

1. Discuss with your child his/her favorite parts, any sad parts, fun parts, or whatever might be appropriate to the story.
2. If your child really liked the book, ask him/her if he/she would want to read it again.

Bibliography of Selected Articles and Books

Alvermann, D. E. (1991). The Discussion Web: A graphic aid for learning across the curriculum. *The Reading Teacher, 45* (2), 92–99.

Arter, J. A. (1990). Using portfolios in instruction and assessment. (Report No. TM 016 096). Portland, OR: Northwest Regional Educational Laboratory. (ERIC Document Reproduction Service No. ED 328 586).

Ballard, L. (1992). Portfolios and self-assessment. *English Journal, 81* (2), 46–48.

Barrs, M. (1990). *The Primary Language Record:* Reflection of issues in evaluation. *Language Arts, 67,* 244–253.

Barrs, M., & Laycock, L. (Eds.). (1989). *Testing reading.* London, England: Centre for Language in Primary Education.

Barrs, M., Ellis, S., Hester, H., & Thomas, A. (1988). The Primary Language Record: *Handbook for teachers.* London, England: Centre for Language in Primary Education.

Barrs, M., Ellis, S., Hester, H., & Thomas, A. (1990). *Patterns of learning:* The Primary Language Record *and the national curriculum.* London, England: Centre for Language in Primary Education.

Baskwill, J., & Whitman, P. (1988). *Evaluation: Whole language, whole child.* NY: Scholastic.

Batten, L. (1991, September). School reform accelerates in Vermont; Topping the list: Improved teacher training, higher-ed partnerships, local control. *The Boston Globe,* p. 32.

Bishop, W. (1989). Qualitative evaluation and the conversational writing classroom. *Journal of Teaching Writing,* (special issue), 267–277.

Bunce-Crim, M. (1992, March). Writing evaluation: Picture of a portfolio. *Instructor,* pp. 28–29.

Chapman, C. (1990). *Authentic writing assessment.* (Report No. EDO–TM–90–4). American Institutes for Research, Washington, DC. (ERIC Document Reproduction Service No. ED 328 606).

Clay, M. C. (1979). *The early detection of reading difficulties.* (3rd ed.). Portsmouth, NH: Heinemann.

Cohen, M. (1990, January). Standardized tests challenged again. *The Boston Globe,* p. B91.

Cooper, C. R. (1977). Holistic evaluation of writing. In C.R. Cooper & L. Odell (Eds.). *Evaluating writing: Describing, measuring, judging* (pp. 3–31). Urbana, IL: National Council of Teachers of English.

Cooper, W., & Brown, B. J. (1992). Using portfolios to empower student writers. *English Journal, 81* (2), 40–45.

De Fina, A. A., Anstendig, L. L., & De Lawter, K. (1991). Alternative integrated reading/writing assessment and curriculum design. *Journal of Reading, 34* (5), 354–359.

Edelsky, C., Altwerger, B., & Flores, B. (1991). *Whole language: What's the difference?* Portsmouth, NH: Heinemann.

Elbow, P., & Belanoff, P. (1986). Portfolios as a substitute for proficiency examinations. *College Composition and Communication, 37* (3), 336–339.

Fiderer, A., Abelove, J., Anders, E., Berger, L., Citron, E., D'Amore, J., Hayter, M., & Huttar, E. (1991). *A language arts portfolio handbook: Alternative assessment strategies for K–5 teachers.* (Available from Scarsdale Public School System, Scarsdale, NY.)

Flood, J., & Lapp, D. (1989). Reporting reading progress: A comparison portfolio for parents. *The Reading Teacher, 42* (7), 508–514.

Flood, J., & Lapp, D. (1991, December). *The beliefs and practices of teachers' use of portfolio assessment in elementary schools.* Paper presented at the meeting of the National Reading Conference, Palm Springs, CA.

Ford, M. P., & Ohlhausen, M. M. (1991, December). *Portfolio assessment in teacher education courses: Impact on students' beliefs, attitudes, and habits.* Paper presented at the meeting of the National Reading Conference, Palm Springs, CA.

Fredericks, A. D., & Rasinski, T. V. (1990) Whole language and parents: Natural partners. *The Reading Teacher, 43* (9), 692–693.

Fredericks, A. D., & Rasinski, T. V. (1990) Involving parents in the assessment process. *The Reading Teacher, 44* (4), 346–349.

Freire, P. (1989). *Pedagogy of the oppressed.* NY: Continuum.

Gable, R. A., Hendrickson, J. M., & Meeks, J. W. (1988). Assessing spelling errors of special needs students. *The Reading Teacher, 42* (2), 112–117.

Gomez, M. L., Graue, M. E., & Bloch, M. N. (1991). Reassessing portfolio assessment: Rhetoric and reality. *Language Arts, 68* (8), 620–628.

Goodman, K. (1986). *What's whole in whole language?* Portsmouth, NH: Heinemann.

Goodman, K., Goodman, Y., & Hood, W. (1988). *The whole language evaluation book.* Portsmouth, NH: Heinemann.

Goodman, Y., Watson, D., & Burke, C. (1987). *Reading Miscue Inventory: Alternate procedures.* NY: Richard C. Owen.

Herter, R. J. (1991). Writing portfolios: Alternatives to testing. *English Journal, 80* (1), 90–91.

Jasmine, J. (1992). *Portfolio assessment for your whole language classroom.* Huntington Beach, CA: Teacher Created Materials, Inc.

Johns, J. L. (1990). *Literacy portfolios.* (Report No. CS 010 074). DeKalb, IL: Northern Illinois University, Reading Clinic. (ERIC Document Reproduction Service No. ED 319 020).

Jongsma, K. S. (1989). Portfolio assessment. *The Reading Teacher, 43* (3), 264–265.

Koklanaris, M. (1991, November). Fairfax report cards yield to "portfolios." *The Washington Times,* p. B1.

Lamme, L. L., & Hysmith, C. (1991). One school's adventure into portfolio assessment. *Language Arts, 68* (8), 629–640.

Lipa, S. E., Harlin, R. P., & Phelps, S. (1991, December). *Portfolio assessment: Diagnostic implications.* Paper presented at the meeting of the National Reading Conference, Palm Springs, CA.

Madden, L. (1988). Improve reading attitudes of poor readers through cooperative reading teams. *The Reading Teacher, 42* (3), 194–199.

Maria, K. (1989). Developing disadvantaged children's background knowledge interactively. *The Reading Teacher, 42* (4), 296–300.

Mathews, J. K. (1990). From computer management to portfolio assessment. *The Reading Teacher, 43* (6), 420–421.

McKenna, M. C., & Kear, D. J. (1990). Measuring attitude toward reading: A new tool for teachers. *The Reading Teacher, 43* (9), 626–639.

Newman, J. M. (Ed.). (1985). *Whole language: theory in use.* Portsmouth, NH: Heinemann.

Nolan, T. E. (1991). Self-questioning and prediction: Combining metacognitive strategies. *Journal of Reading, 35* (2), 132–138.

Partridge, S. (1990). Assessing students' writing in the 1990s: A discussion. (Report No. CS 212 ;462). (ERIC Document Reproduction Service No. ED 322 512).

Paulson, F. L., & Paulson, P. R. How *do portfolios measure up? A cognitive model for assessing portfolios.* (Report No. TM 015 516). Union, WA: North-west Evaluation Association. (ERIC Document Reproduction Service No. ED 324 329).

Paulson, F. L., Paulson, P. R., & Meyer, C. A. (1991). What makes a portfolio a portfolio? *Educational Leadership, 48* (5), 60–63.

Peters, C. W. (1991). You can't have authentic assessment without authentic content. *The Reading Teacher, 44* (8), 590–591.

Probst, R. (1988). *Response and analysis: Teaching literature in junior and senior high school.* Portsmouth, NH: Heinemann.

Purves, A. C. (1992). Reflections on research and assessment in written composition. *Research in the Teaching of English, 26* (1), 108–122.

Rayer, J. K. (1991). *Portfolio assessment for early childhood educators.* (Available from Mainz American Elementary School, Box 524 HHC-USMCA, APO New York, NY 09185.)

Rhodes, L. K., & Nathenson-Mejia, S. (1992), Anecdotal records: A powerful tool for ongoing literacy assessment. *The Reading Teacher, 45* (7), 502–509.

Ringler, L. H. (1991). *Informal assessment of narrative text.* Unpublished manuscript.

Roe, M. F. (1991, December). *Portfolios: From mandate to implementation.* Paper presented at the meeting of the National Reading Conference, Palm Springs, CA.

Rosenblatt, L. (1978). *The reader, the text, the poem: The transactional theory of the literary work.* Carbondale, IL: Southern Illinois University.

Rousculp, E. E., & Maring, G. H. (1990). *Writing portfolios for a community of learners in a content area reading course.* (Report No. CS 212 541). Pull-man, WA: Washington State University, Department of Elementary and Secondary Education. (ERIC Document Reproduction Service No. ED 324 687).

Rousculp, E. E., & Maring, G. H. (1992). Portfolios for a community of learners. *Journal of Reading, 35* (5), 378–385.

Sharp, Q. Q. (1989). *Evaluation: Whole language checklists for evaluating your children for grades K to 6.* NY: Scholastic.

Simmons, J. (1990). Portfolios as large-scale assessment. *Language Arts*, *67*, 262–268.

Test publishers caution policymakers on recommendations for new education standards and testing. (February, 1992). *U. S. Newswire*.

Tierney, R. J., Carter, M. A., & Desai, L. E. (1991). *Portfolio assessment in the reading-writing classroom*. Norwood, MA: Christopher-Gordon Publishers, Inc.

Valencia, S. (1990). A portfolio approach to classroom reading assessment: The whys, whats, and hows. *The Reading Teacher*, *43* (4), 338–340.

Valencia, S., McGinley, W., & Pearson, P. D. (1990). *Assessing reading and writing: Building a more complete picture for middle school assessment*. (Report No. CS 010 116). Champaign, WIL: University of Illinois at Urbana-Champaign, Center for the Study of Reading. (ERIC Document Reproduction Service No. ED 320 121).

Valeri-Gold, M., Olson, J. R., Deming, M. P. (1991). Portfolios: Collaborative authentic assessment opportunities for college developmental learners. *Journal of Reading*, *35*(4), 298–305.

Weaver, C. (1988). *Reading process and practice from socio-psycholinguistics to whole language*. Portsmouth, NH: Heinemann.

Werner, P. H. (1992). Integrated Assessment System. *Journal of Reading*, *35* (5), 416–418.

White, E. (1985). *Teaching and assessing writing*. San Francisco, CA: Jossey-Bass.

Winograd, P., Paris, S., & Bridge, C. (1991). Improving the assessment of literacy. *The Reading Teacher*, *45* (2), 108–116.

Wolf, K. P. (1991, December). *The influence of portfolio assessment on classroom instruction in elementary literacy*. Paper presented at the meeting of the National Reading Conference, Palm Springs, CA.

Wolf, K. P., Athanases, S., & Chin, E. (1988). Designing portfolios for the assessment of elementary literacy teaching: Work-in-progress. (Report No. CS 009 495). Stanford, CA: Stanford University, Teacher Assessment Project, School of Education. (ERIC Document Reproduction Service No. ED 302 842).

Yancey, K. B. (Ed.). (1992). *Portfolios in the writing classroom: An introduction*. Urbana, IL: National Council of Teachers of English.